P[~~~~]

St[~~~~]nson, [~~~~]l.

A [~~~~] to the
[~~~~] novel in
B[~~~~]

DATE DUE			
OCT 26 '93			

A Reader's Guide to the Twentieth-Century Novel in Britain

For Caroline, Ron, and Vassiliki;
and for Olga

A Reader's Guide to the Twentieth-Century Novel in Britain

Randall Stevenson

The University Press of Kentucky

Published by The University Press of Kentucky

Scholarly publisher for the Commonwealth,
serving Bellarmine College, Berea College, Centre
College of Kentucky, Eastern Kentucky University,
The Filson Club, Georgetown College, Kentucky
Historical Society, Kentucky State University,
Morehead State University, Murray State University,
Northern Kentucky University, Transylvania University,
University of Kentucky, University of Louisville,
and Western Kentucky University.

Editorial and Sales Offices: Lexington, Kentucky 40508–4008

Library of Congress Cataloging-in-Publication Data
are available from the publisher.

Printed and bound in Great Britain

ISBN 0–8131–1857–3
ISBN 0–8131–0823–3 (pbk)

Contents

Introduction

This study's title raises some questions: preliminary discussion of them may help to clarify the scope and strategy of what follows.

Readers, first of all. What readers? This is a question more sharply – sometimes soberingly – significant for twentieth-century novelists than for most of their predecessors. For much of the nineteenth century, novels admired for their literary quality were also fairly widely read. This broad readership for literary fiction, however, did not always survive into the twentieth century. From its very beginning, a resulting uneasiness is sometimes apparent in the work of its more serious and ambitious authors: in Joseph Conrad's *Lord Jim* (1900), for example, which may have been – for reasons Chapter One will discuss – the first genuinely modern novel published in Britain. Much of Conrad's story takes the form of a long after-dinner monologue, supposedly delivered by his narrator Marlow to a circle of largely silent and rather patient listeners. This means of telling the story might be seen as a figuration of Conrad's anxiety about the chances of finding an actual audience for his work – as an attempt to create within the fiction itself an audience which he suspected might not otherwise exist for it, or exist on a rather limited scale. As several critics have explained,[1] changes in the economics of publishing and the expansion of literacy in the late nineteenth century made it easier – if not entirely rewarding – for novelists to indulge, like Conrad, their preference for unusual, sometimes challenging forms of fiction. A larger overall market for books by the turn of the century made it possible to appeal not to the whole public, as Conrad's predecessors often had, but only to limited sections of it.

Other writers at the time began to profit – artistically if not financially – from this new situation. As Chapter One explains, Henry James insisted on the artistic qualities of the novel – and described at length how best these could be sustained – while selling many fewer copies of his own books than writers such as H.G. Wells to whom he considered himself artistically superior. Working slightly earlier than Joseph Conrad, James is probably the first novelist in English whose writing has been widely admired for its literary and artistic qualities despite being largely ignored by the reading public, at least when it first appeared. This situation, however, grows more common later in the century. Virginia Woolf is one of the most admired and influential of twentieth-century authors, with views as strong as James's on the artistic responsibilities of the novelist and the failure of some of her contemporaries to fulfil them, yet she records in her diary that her best hope for her novel *Mrs Dalloway* (1925) – on the basis of earlier figures – was that it might sell 2,000 copies. Only later in the century has the gap between critical or artistic and popular success narrowed once again. Though technological advances have redirected the widest audience for narrative towards video, television and film, an author in the 1990s whose novel wins a prize for literary merit can reasonably hope that it may also sell several hundred thousand copies.

This gap between artistic and popular success throughout much of the twentieth century has sometimes been held to explain another development specific to the age – the great expansion in literary criticism, including commentary on fiction. Some mediation is required to make more available the pleasures, vision or ideas of writing thought to be worthwhile literature yet lacking ease or immediacy of appeal, and this is one of the needs criticism may answer. At any rate, at least until recently, novel criticism has habitually concentrated on material whose qualities – of sophistication, subtlety, profundity, shapeliness, vision, multi-layeredness or whatever – seem to qualify it as literature, while also demanding further discussion and elucidation. The present study does not particularly seek to break this critical habit. Where possible, however, it does try to indicate some of the places occupied in twentieth-century imagination by the sci-fi, spy stories, detective novels and other thrillers now often placed critically in the sub-class of 'genre fiction'. Additionally, since part of popular fiction's appeal is often owed to the success with which it contains contemporary problems and preoccupations, several chapters also make use of its capacity to reveal the temper and outlook of its age.

On the whole, however, this remains a guide to the literary fiction of the twentieth century. Length is a further limit on the range of work it considers. A shortish study cannot be exhaustive: the pages that follow could be fairly well filled simply by listing all the twentieth-century novels that might still be worth reading. Several whole books which are devoted to this kind of list appear in the Bibliography, and the Further Reading suggested at the end of each chapter includes detailed, comprehensive studies of individual periods. In tracing the nature of the novel, age by age, the chapters that follow do try to include not only the major authors of the century but also as many as possible of the less well-known, though sometimes by discussing only one or a few of their novels (where appropriate, publishing details of the works referred to appear in the Bibliography). Throughout, however, priority is given to pre-senting patterns rather than particulars – to tracing and illustrating the main outlines of the novel's development, rather than assessing *all* the authors who may have contributed to them. Readers inclined to lament the absence of a cherished novel – or even a whole novelist – should find instead a pattern within the century's various periods into which they may insert omitted items for themselves.

These patterns and outlines are generally shown shaped by two factors: literary history and, ultimately, history itself. Discussing the first of these in her essay 'Modern Fiction' (1919), Virginia Woolf remarks that

> we do not come to write better; all that we can be said to do is to keep moving, now a little in this direction, now in that, but with a circular tendency should the whole course of the track be viewed from a sufficiently lofty pinnacle.[2]

On the contrary, at many points of the twentieth century writers *have* assumed that they could write better than at least their immediate predecessors – despite Woolf's apparent modesty, much of her essay is dedicated to showing how this might be achieved for her contemporaries and herself. As a result, many of the century's individual periods are distinguished by sets of rejections or reactions made by generations of writers who successively discard the influence of their elders, rather like generations of children. Since some generations react in their turn against the rejections made by the preceding one, the progress of literary history is at times, as Woolf suggests, rather circular – writers in the thirties and fifties, for example, sometimes returning to the example of the Edwardians. There are, nevertheless, also phases of more radical change, such as Woolf's own – the modernist period examined in Chapter Two, whose new influences are traceable in much of the rest of the century.

At any rate, literary history in the twentieth century – as no doubt in others – most often develops in processes of adoption, adaptation or rejection of existing forms and styles. What determines these processes, however, is not only the arbitrary or adolescent whims or disdains of succeeding generations of authors, but also – as Woolf suggests in 'Modern Fiction' and several other essays – the nature of the times in which they live. Only a very limited history of twentieth-century fiction would fail to pay some attention to the history of the century itself: this study, however, goes further, showing that while almost every novelist chooses from – or at least chooses to redevelop – an existing repertoire of possibilities, it is the shapes and tensions of contemporary society and history which govern their choice. Much more than merely the themes and stories of the novel are affected in this way by history – by the politics, society and pressure of events in their time. Many novelists throughout the century do present or discuss its history directly – George Orwell's *Coming up for Air* (1939), for example, looks so closely at the Edwardian age that it is thoroughly useful for analysis of this period in Chapter One. But history also affects modern fiction which has little explicit connection to it. Its processes insert themselves into the form and imagination even of novels – such as some of those considered in Chapters Two and Four – apparently most concerned simply to evade or ignore its stresses. A good deal of the interest of twentieth-century writing lies in the prospect it offers of the imagination twisting and turning, this way and that, trying to shape in new forms and mythologies some of the consolations and coherence the age itself has seemed so conspicuously to lack. It is this interest which this study principally seeks to communicate.

A reader's guide, then, to the literary novel, in Britain, in the context of its times. To 'the novel in Britain'? Why not just say 'to British fiction'? The four authors mentioned so far help to provide an answer. Two of them, Joseph Conrad and Henry James, arrived in Britain only late in life; Orwell was born abroad and spent some of his formative years in Burma; and although she was a Londoner by birth and domicile, even Virginia Woolf found herself significantly 'alien' to her home society in ways further discussed in Chapter Six. As such mixed backgrounds suggest, categorising literature in terms of the origin or nationality of its authors has been difficult through-out the century: it is growing more so in the increasingly international context of life and writing at its end. By the year 2000, if not before, English Literature may find itself renamed for purposes of study as Literature in English, with one of its defining features the language of texts, rather than simply the nationality of their authors.

Meanwhile, discussing 'the novel in Britain' is not an ideal compromise. It offers little rationale for the inclusion of some Irish writers – especially the Paris-based ones, James Joyce and Samuel Beckett – other than the impossibility of excluding from *any* assessment of twentieth-century fiction in English authors who have been so comprehensively influential upon it. Scottish and Welsh writers also belong in their own way to traditions quite distinct from the English one. And yet it is the conscious-ness of having to share a language and – in the case of the Scots, Welsh and Northern Irish – a political system with a more powerful, influential English neighbour which is actually responsible in part for shaping these traditions, and even their feelings of distinctness. Awareness of a broader system accen-tuates the sense of the local, separate and specific. As Chapter Six discusses, this kind of double awareness – of the particular along with the general – has been throughout the century a difficult but fruitful one for writers in Britain, which provides a context of provocatively conflicting national and cultural identities. In this way, 'the novel in Britain' can still provide a worthwhile means of categorisation, especially if used loosely rather than to imply only homogeneity, or much autonomy from external influences. Like any account of the weather in Britain, an assessment of the twentieth-century novel in Britain needs to show broad systems sometimes moving across the country from overseas, and local variations sometimes of more significance than pictures of the area as a whole. It will also have to consider adverse comparisons sometimes made with conditions in continental Europe, and elsewhere.

Of all the terms in the title, the twentieth century is the least problematic, definable simply with dates. It is nevertheless curious to find the novelist Compton Mackenzie recording a contemporary assumption that the last year of the nineteenth century was actually 1900, and that the twentieth began only in January 1901. More certain agreement might be reached that – with luck – the century will not end where this study is obliged to, in the early 1990s. Some of the patterns discussed in recent writing, however, are probably strong enough to continue shaping fiction up to the millennium. They are considered in this way in Chapter Six, although the end of the century will also, surely, experience a sense of conclusion and fresh beginning – conscious or unconscious – sharp enough to affect fiction in ways which cannot yet be easily predicted. In any case, patterns in recent fiction can be identified only rather more provisionally than in the writing of the earlier part of the century. In Woolf's terms, there is still no pinnacle distant or lofty enough to allow a broad or wholly clear perspective on this part of the 'track' of the twentieth century. Accordingly, more particulars – rather more authors and texts – are mentioned in considering the past thirty years than in discussing earlier periods. This also introduces readers more fully to areas generally less thoroughly studied than their predecessors. Showing the recent and contemporary as a legacy of the now-established classics of the twentieth century – those of the modernist period in particular – is a priority of the guide as a whole.

The fiction of a whole century – or even a mere ninety-two years – is a big subject, and I am grateful to many people who have helped with it. Jackie Jones has been an admirably patient, thoughtful editor throughout. At various points I have relied on the advice, ideas and encouragement of Clare Brennan, David Denby, Iona Gogeanu, Jane Goldman, Susanne Greenhalgh, Corina Iordache, Nana Kolocotroni, Drew Milne, Colin Nicholson, Gavin Wallace and Peter Womack. For vision of life as well as literature I have owed most in recent years to those named in the dedication; and as always to Sarah Carpenter.

1   *Elephant and Sandcastle*

The Edwardian Years

Back in 1900 . . . I'd been breathing real air . . . it was a good world to live in . . .

Before the war, and especially before the Boer War, it was summer all the year round . . . a hot afternoon in the great green juicy meadows round the town . . .

1911, 1912, 1913. I tell you it was a good time to be alive . . . The white dusty road stretching out between the chestnut trees, the smell of nightstocks, the green pools under the willows . . . the feeling inside you, the feeling of not being in a hurry and not being frightened . . .

The spring of 1914 . . .

What's the use of saying one oughtn't to be sentimental about 'before the war'? I *am* sentimental about it . . . It's quite true that if you look back on any special period of time you tend to remember the pleasant bits . . . But it's also true that people then had something that we haven't got now . . .

What was it that people had in those days? A feeling of security, even when they weren't secure. More exactly, it was a feeling of continuity . . . what they didn't know was that the order of things could change . . . A settled period, a period when civilisation seems to stand on its four legs like an elephant . . . they didn't feel the ground they stood on shifting under their feet . . .

The old English order of life couldn't change . . . They lived at the end of an epoch, when everything was dissolving into a sort of ghastly flux, and they didn't know it. They thought it was eternity . . .

Then came the end of July . . . then suddenly the posters everywhere:

GERMAN ULTIMATUM. FRANCE MOBILIZING . . .

ENGLAND DECLARES WAR ON GERMANY.
(pp.34, 37, 102, 103, 104, 106–9)

The nostalgia in George Orwell's *Coming up for Air* (1939) has much to reveal about the years before the First World War – usually referred to as the Edwardian period, though Edward VII actually died in 1910 – and about the way they have come to be perceived later in the century. In later periods of greater historical stress – such as the desolate years after the First World War, or the time of the Second – novelists have often, like Orwell, looked back on the Edwardian era as a lost Eden of peace and stability; a period when a sunny security was enjoyed for the last time in British history. As Orwell indicates – and as will be discussed further below – this idea of an Edwardian Eden is clearly a sentimental one, constructed from memories only of 'the pleasant bits'. And yet there is some truth in the summery picture of this time, which at least offered more promising raw material – relatively more 'pleasant bits' – than subsequent eras to novelists' myths of peace and happiness lost in the past. The opening years of the century genuinely were, in some ways, 'a good time to be alive' in Britain, whose situation, both domestically and internationally, did offer some promise of security, continuity and hope for the future. By the time the First World War broke out in August 1914, Britain had enjoyed nearly a hundred years of almost continuous peace with her European neighbours. The latter part of the nineteenth and the early twentieth century also enjoyed the fruits of an almost continuous advance in British Imperial power. By 1900, the Empire had grown to cover 13 million square miles, and to rule nearly 400 million people. This created a secure source of raw materials, an expanding market for British manufacturing, and even, in some quarters, a context for idealism. The novelist Arthur Conan Doyle, for example, claimed in 1900 that

The Imperial Government has always taken an honourable and philanthropic view of the rights of the native . . .

The British flag under our best administrators will mean clean government, honest laws, liberty and equality to all men.[1]

On the domestic scene, there were genuine hopes that the near future might see a more equable, rational society – even a perfect one – created by better administration, the progress of education and of science and technology, and the possibilities of socialism and of universal suffrage. Utopian visions or ideas were often expressed at the time: by H.G. Wells, for example, in his study *A Modern Utopia* (1905), or in the ideal state of free love and communism shown at the end of his novel *In the Days of the Comet* (1906). Even among those who were unconvinced by utopias – or believed it would require something as magical as Wells's visiting comet to create one – the 'feeling of continuity' Orwell mentions might have promised an acceptable future based simply on the apparent stability of the past and the present age. During the Victorian era, at least until its latter years, the institutions of church, monarchy, state and family helped contribute to the consoling sense recorded in *Coming up for Air* that

> the year's 1900 . . . Vicky's at Windsor, God's in his heaven, Christ's on the cross, Jonah's in the whale . . . not doing anything exactly, just existing, keeping their appointed places. (p.34)

Yet however easy it might have been in 1900 to think of everything keeping its appointed place, there were also ways in which it grew significantly less so in the years that followed. However solidly stable the Edwardian elephant may have appeared, there were also signs at the time, as Orwell indicates, that it actually had its feet planted on shifting ground – on sands shifting and dissolving in the long, withdrawing tide of faiths and assumptions that had sustained the Victorians. This dissolution was probably more visible to the Edwardians than Orwell suggests, at least to contemporary authors. It is worth looking generally at the ways in which the fiction of the period reflects some of its uncertainties, before going on to consider how the major Edwardian authors came to terms with an age in which change and crisis increasingly eroded feelings of continuity.

More or less coinciding with the end of the century, the death of Queen Victoria particularly focused contemporary feelings of change. It released in the Edwardian period accumulated uneasiness with the manners and assumptions that had developed during a reign stretching back more than sixty years to Victoria's accession in 1837. In *The Old Wives' Tale* (1908), Arnold Bennett criticises what he calls the 'vast, arid Victorian expanse of years' (p.182). In his radical avant-garde journal *Blast* (1914) Wyndham Lewis was still more determined to 'BLAST years 1837 to 1900 . . . BOURGEOIS VICTORIAN VISTAS . . . GLOOMY VICTORIAN CIRCUS' (pp.18–19). Such criticism had some of its roots much earlier, within the Victorian period itself. Samuel Butler began writing his semi-autobiographical novel *The Way of all Flesh* as long before as the 1870s: when it was eventually published in 1903, it powerfully coincided with wider Edwardian resentments of the century just completed – of the stultifying effects of Victorian education and social institutions, and, in particular, of the constraints of Victorian family life. Similar views of the Victorian family and its tyrannical patriarchs appear in Bennett's *Anna of the Five Towns* (1902) – its heroine suffering from a father of 'sinister and formidable individuality' (p.30) – and in Edmund Gosse's *Father and Son* (1907). Comparable criticism figures in George Douglas Brown's *The House with the Green Shutters* (1901), in which the narrow, tyrannical outlook of the central figure is reduplicated and amplified by the townsfolk who surround him. The same kind of narrow, restrictive Scottish community is examined in J. McDougall Hay's *Gillespie* (1914); in part, like Brown's novel, a riposte to the 'kailyard' fiction of S.R. Crockett and J.M. Barrie, which created in the late nineteenth and early twentieth century an implausibly sweet and idealised image of rural Scotland.

As well as criticising Victorian attitudes and family constraints, Samuel Butler suggests in *The Way of all Flesh* a means of escaping them; of creating a freer life shaped by the influences of literature and art. Such attitudes and possibilities also appear in some of the *Bildungsromans* – a form popular with the Victorians – which continued to appear in great numbers in the Edwardian period. These include Arnold Bennett's *Clayhanger* series (1910– 18); H.G. Wells's *Tono-Bungay* (1909); Compton Mackenzie's *Sinister Street* (1913–14); D.H. Lawrence's *Sons and Lovers* (1913);

and James Joyce's *A Portrait of the Artist as a Young Man* (1916). Tracing the personal education and development towards maturity of a single, central character, in one way these *Bildungsromans* suggest the survival from the Victorian era of the 'feeling of continuity' Orwell describes – of faith in the evolving coherence of the individual life in time. Yet some of these novels differ markedly from their Victorian predecessors. Whereas Charles Dickens's *David Copperfield* (1849–50), for example, follows its hero to the point where he has become a successful family man, comfortably established in his society, novels such as *Sons and Lovers* or *A Portrait of the Artist as a Young Man* end with their central figures in lonely situations of partial exclusion or even contemplated exile from family and community. Any personal stability or maturity they achieve results much less from integration with their society than from development as an artist, aloof and ironically detached from it. Especially as it appears in Compton Mackenzie's *Sinister Street*, such interest in art also follows on from the critique of Victorian manners and earnestness established in the doctrine of art for art's sake and the decadence and dandyism at the end of the nineteenth century. Such attitudes of aestheticism continue to shape some fiction later in the twentieth century, especially the work of Ronald Firbank in the twenties. When they first appeared in the 1890s they were probably clearest not in the novel but in drama – in the plays of Oscar Wilde, and particularly *The Importance of Being Earnest* (1895), which shows a kind of ultimate defeat of the Victorian family ruler, ludicrously personified in Lady Bracknell.

Doubts about Victorian family life naturally extended into criticism of the values on which it was based, part of a wider contemporary scepticism about the religious faith which had sustained the Victorians. Like Vicky, no longer at Windsor, God Himself seemed more and more to have lost his 'appointed place' in the secure scheme of things described in *Coming up for Air*. Samuel Butler saw Christianity discredited by evolutionary theory: many others in the late nineteenth century also began to consider the foundations of religion undermined by the evidence of Charles Darwin in *The Origin of Species* (1859). This scepticism rapidly advanced in the early twentieth century. H.G. Wells pointed in 1911 to 'an enormous criticism going on of the faiths upon which men's lives and associations are based, and of every standard and rule of conduct'.[2] This criticism is illustrated by some of Wells's own fiction. When despair forces his hero in *Tono-Bungay*, George Ponderevo, to seek 'salvation . . . something to hold on to' (pp.167–8), he does not turn to the church, but considers instead the other new faiths of the age: socialism, science, and – his ultimate choice – the power created by sophisticated engineering. Joyce's hero in *A Portrait of the Artist as a Young Man*, and to some extent Mackenzie's in *Sinister Street*, likewise find in art an alternative to strong attachments to the church.

As the Introduction suggested, contemporary feelings and anxieties of this kind are often still more clearly represented in popular fiction. Guy Thorne's hugely successful *When it was Dark: The story of a great conspiracy* (1904) reflects both the sense of a general decline in faith and anxieties about its likely consequence. The novel laments that after Darwin 'scientific criticism of the Scriptures undermined the faith of weaker . . . minds' (p.9) and regrets the contemporary Huxleyan view of 'religion as an unwelcome restraint upon liberty of thought' (p.205). In response, Thorne presents in admonitory terms the terrible results of a conspiracy to discredit the truth of the Resurrection: world-wide outrages against morality; wars ruining the British Empire; and – most alarmingly of all – collapse of the world's stock markets and financial systems.

When it was Dark reflects one phase of Edwardian uncertainty: another is also apparent in popular fiction in a great wave of invasion novels published at the time. These had begun to appear under the shadow of shifting balances of power after the Franco–Prussian war in 1871, but multiplied rapidly in the Edwardian period in response to intensifying international confrontation and an arms race which saw the construction of more and more dreadnought warships. William Le Queux, for example, leaves readers in no doubt about the relevance to this situation of his novel *The Invasion of 1910: With a full account of the siege of London* (1906). His preface explains that 'to arouse our country to a sense of its own lamentable insecurity is the object of this volume' (pp.ix–x), Le Queux adding that it was written in consultation with the leading military strategists of the day. Like Erskine Childers in his popular thriller *The Riddle of the Sands*

(1903), or H.G. Wells, whose magical comet turns up just in time to prevent a European conflict, Le Queux chooses Germany as the likeliest aggressor in a future war. Such expectations were widely shared at the time: as Orwell remarks in *Coming up for Air*,

> People began to say rather vaguely that this here German Emperor was getting too big for his boots and 'it' (meaning war with Germany) was 'coming some time'. (p.98)

This growing sense of the possibility – even necessity – of a European war further undermined contemporary feelings of security and continuity, and in the end made the events of July and August 1914 perhaps less of a complete surprise than *Coming up for Air* suggests.

Le Queux's anxieties accurately anticipated a future conflict: they were also the result of a previous one, the Boer War at the turn of the century. 'History tells us', Le Queux's preface emphasises, 'that an Empire which cannot defend its own possessions must inevitably perish' (p.v) – very much the lesson inflicted by Boer successes in the Transvaal late in 1899. These ensured that Britain entered the twentieth century in a position of particular doubt concerning its Empire, Arthur Conan Doyle describing the experience of December 1899 as 'the blackest one known during our generation . . . the indirect effects in the way of loss of prestige . . . were incalculable'.[3] Though the Boer War was eventually won, it undermined the idea of British omnipotence, and challenged faith in the values on which the Empire was supposedly based. The late twentieth century has grown only too familiar with wars undertaken to secure deposits of a natural resource – in this case the gold of the Transvaal – or involving concentration camps and the massive use of propaganda. All this was more of a shock in 1900, making it more difficult to share Conan Doyle's belief in the natural intertwining of the British flag with 'honest laws, liberty and equality to all men'. It also became more difficult to write the kind of adventure stories – popular in the late nineteenth century – in which authors such as Rider Haggard and Conan Doyle sought to propagate the virtues of courage, loyalty, honour and daring necessary for the maintenance of empire. Conan Doyle also found, in the new century, his Sherlock Holmes partly supplanted by G.K. Chesterton's Father Brown (in stories such as *The Innocence of Father Brown*, 1911) as the age's favourite detective. In various forms, the imperial adventure story nevertheless did survive: in Rudyard Kipling's *Kim* (1901), for example; in Conan Doyle's own *The Lost World* (1912); and in John Buchan's *Prester John* (1910) and *The Thirty-Nine Steps* (1915). Buchan's fast-paced, patriotic tales of action and intrigue also helped create a pattern and a market for later generations of spy and adventure stories such as Ian Fleming's James Bond novels.

The major Edwardian writers, however, were often doubtful of the values of empire, and sometimes specifically sceptical of the light literature and adventure stories which helped to support them. In *The Good Soldier* (1915), Ford Madox Ford's hero Edward Ashburnham is described as 'full of the big words, courage, loyalty, honour, constancy', and as 'an English gentleman . . . whose mind was compounded of indifferent poems and novels' (pp.31, 229). Ford exposes an inevitable gap between these inflated ideals and some of Ashburnham's actual behaviour. In *Chance* (1913), Joseph Conrad complains that 'we are the creatures of our light literature much more than is generally suspected' (p.241), and he also examines in *Lord Jim* (1900) the dubious influence of the 'light holiday literature' (p.11) whose images of remote, romantic adventure first lead his hero to a career at sea. Often exotic and colourful itself, *Lord Jim* is a kind of sceptical reworking of the imperial adventure, showing how disastrously Jim's romantic self-image encounters the harsh challenges of an actual life at sea. 'Dreams and the success of his imaginary achievements' (p.21) do not prevent him from abandoning ship, betraying both immediate trust and the more exalted values he hoped to embody. Seeming splendidly sound and reliable, yet deeply responsible for deceit and betrayal, both Jim and Ashburnham are Edwardian hollow men, emblematic of the superficial solidity but actual emptiness or uncertainty of contemporary values.

These values and their relation to the Empire are also examined in Conrad's *Heart of Darkness* (1902), supposedly narrated, like *Lord Jim*, by the garrulous mariner Marlow. For many years a British merchant seaman, Conrad knew some of the processes of empire at first hand and drew on this experience in the novel. *Heart of Darkness* is not entirely critical of empire, or not at any rate the British version of it. If anything, this is supported by Marlow's approval of the 'vast amount of red' on the map – 'good to see at any time, because one knows that some real work is done there' (p.36). Conrad, however, remains concerned with what happens to imperial ambitions bereft of controlling ideas, morals and a worthwhile sense of purpose. Imperial conquest, Marlow comments, is 'not a pretty thing . . . what redeems it is the idea only . . . an unselfish belief in the idea' (p.32). Without this, foreign ambitions are only 'brute force': the kind of robbery with violence in which Marlow comes to feel 'the Company' he works for is principally engaged. His doubts are confirmed when his journey into the African interior eventually leads him to the celebrated Kurtz. Supposedly 'an emissary of pity, and science, and progress . . . the cause intrusted to us by Europe' (p.55), Kurtz proves to be another hollow man: 'hollow at the core', overtaken by barbarity, and revered by 'the Company' largely for his discovery of 'something that is really profitable' (pp.97, 110).

Conrad's criticism of imperial ambition is still sharper in fiction written – unlike *Heart of Darkness* – after the Boer War. In *Nostromo* (1904), redeeming ideas seem still more tenuous or untenable, and profit a still more inescapable motive. Though Charles Gould and his idealistic wife set out full of naïve inspiration – backed by money from the United States – they find in the South American republic of Costaguana that 'there is no peace and no rest in the development of material interests' (p.419). Pursuit of these interests eventually destroys the stability of the country and the lives of many of its inhabitants, as well as the initial idealism of the Goulds themselves, leaving only 'the religion of silver and iron' (p.71) in control of their mining company. *Nostromo* offers in this way one of the fullest examinations of an anxiety central to the Edwardian age – that in default of religious faith or other systems of value, an unchecked capitalism, a rapidly advancing materialism, had become the only ruling forces in contemporary society.

Reflected by Conrad in the context of empire, this dominant anxiety also appears in contemporary fiction's vision of the ordering of British society at home. Within Britain – as several contemporary surveys of widespread and appalling poverty emphasised – the affluence fostered by the Industrial Revolution and extended by Empire was neither justly distributed nor obviously directed by commitment to anything other than further extension of itself. As George Ponderevo complains in Wells's *Tono-Bungay*, in 'the whole of this modern mercantile investing civilisation . . . ultimate aims [are] vague and forgotten' (p.186). To varying degrees, concerns of this kind are addressed by most of the major Edwardian novelists – by E.M. Forster, John Galsworthy and Arnold Bennett as well as by Conrad, and most directly and regularly by H.G. Wells himself. Wells's determination to deal with immediate social issues underlies his abandonment of the 'scientific romances' (science fiction) – such as *The Time Machine* (1895), *The War of the Worlds* (1898) and *The First Men in the Moon* (1901) – which had occupied him up to the turn of the century. Even in these novels, political or social issues are often present in an oblique form – in the vision in *The Time Machine* of a future world divided between a ruling and a slave class, or the uneasiness about imperial conquest which can be seen in *The War of the Worlds*. In his Edwardian writing, however, Wells seeks a more straightforward assessment of new economic forces, class divisions, and the inequities of contemporary life, generally reflecting these issues in realistic social comedies.

The best of these follow the pattern George Ponderevo suggests in *Tono-Bungay* when he remarks that

Most people in this world . . . have a class, they have a place . . . but there is also another kind of life . . . a miscellaneous tasting of life. One gets hit by some unusual transverse force, one is jerked out of one's stratum and lives crosswise for the rest of the time, and, as it were, in a succession of samples. (p.3)

Wells's heroes often follow the 'other kind of life' Ponderevo defines. Jerked out of their place in one social stratum, they engage in a series of encounters with other strata; a miscellaneous 'succession of samples' of contemporary life which provides what *Tono-Bungay* calls 'remarkable social range . . . [an] extensive cross-section of the British social organism' (p.4). The hero of *The History of Mr Polly* (1910) seeks freedom from the drudgery of his shop in a revealing variety of contexts. Like many of Charles Dickens's characters, the protagonist of *Kipps*

(1905) is an orphan, jerked out of his place by an unexpected inheritance and pitched into a succession of painful, awkward encounters with what the novel calls 'the ruling power of this land, Stupidity' (p.264) – and the class consciousness which is an apparently ineradicable part of it. In the service of his uncle, whose quack medicine takes him from poverty to astonishing wealth, the range of George Ponderevo's own experiences creates a still more panoramic social vision in *Tono-Bungay*. This includes the decline of the almost feudal class system George witnesses in his rural childhood – the 'broad, slow decay of the great social organism of England' (p.52) – and its replacement by a crassly materialist business world, building huge commercial organisations around the hollow promise of advertising and the corrupt machinations of high finance. Under these influences, Britain is shown to have become

> a country hectic with a wasting, aimless fever of trade and money making . . . greedy trade, base profit-seeking, bold advertisement – and kingship and chivalry . . . dead. (pp.323, 325)

The breadth of such concerns makes *Tono-Bungay* at times almost more a survey of 'the Condition of England' – the subject of much contemporary sociological study – than a novel. 'But where has my story got to?' Ponderevo legitimately asks himself in the course of a long analysis of the way London houses 'whole classes . . . in such squalidly unsuitable dwellings' (pp.72-3). The primacy in Wells's work of such sociological interests corresponds with his own view that he would 'rather be called a journalist than an artist'[4] and the opinion stated in *Kipps* that 'the business of a novelist is . . . facts' (p.268).

John Galsworthy's work is principally satire, in which the need for change is implied rather than stated as it often is in Wells's. The conditions of contemporary life which disturbed the two authors are nevertheless similar. Poverty and its effects are examined in Galsworthy's first novel, *The Island Pharisees* (1904). A concern with rampant materialism and the falseness and cruelty of social convention extends throughout his major work, *The Forsyte Saga*. Especially in its first volume, *A Man of Property* (1906), Galsworthy demonstrates the impossibility of true values – or true love – in a world ruled by the Forsytes' obsession with money and property. For example, when Irene Forsyte seeks to escape this world with a lover, she leaves a note for her husband Soames in her jewel case – significantly, this is the one place he is sure to look, since he thinks of her merely as another valuable object, indistinguishable from his other possessions. By continuing to treat her in this way, as a possession and a thrall, he manages to destroy any genuine love or passion she can feel. This and other sad triumphs of the Forsytes' 'sense of property' Galsworthy uses – like Wells's 'samples' – to illustrate problems for the age as a whole. 'A Forsyte is not an uncommon animal,' he comments in the course of the novel, 'there are . . . hundreds out there in the streets' (p.256).

In Arnold Bennett's *Anna of the Five Towns* the heroine's father believes that 'the productivity of capital was . . . the greatest achievement of social progress' (p.109). Like Wells and Galsworthy, Bennett expresses doubts about such contemporary materialism – but also about the possibility of changing it or escaping its consequences. Instead, his fiction often makes conditions created by 'the productivity of capital' seem inevitable and inescapable. Grim, soulless industrial landscapes dominate many of his novels. The setting of *Anna of the Five Towns*, for example, is described as

> One of the fairest spots in Alfred's England, but which is now defaced by the activities of a quarter of a million people. Five contiguous towns . . . mean and forbidding of aspect – sombre, hard-featured, uncouth. (pp.24–5)

Though 'error of destiny' has left sensitive Anna in this 'wrong environment' (p.19), it is one from which – unlike Wells's Kipps – even a substantial legacy cannot help her escape. Instead, in ways learned partly from French writers such as Emile Zola and Guy de Maupassant, Bennett illustrates the inescapable pressure of physical, environmental factors on self and emotion. Such factors are so dominant, and so central to Bennett's interests, that they sometimes seem almost to replace attention to his characters. At one point in *Anna of the Five Towns*, for example, Bennett interrupts for two pages a crucial conversation between Anna and her future husband in order to describe in detail the physical environment in which it takes place.

The same priorities shape one of the best of Bennett's novels, *The Old Wives' Tale*. The author remarks that his heroines Sophia and Constance Baines have 'never been conscious' (p.27) of the physical situation of the Five Towns or its influence on their lives, yet the novel opens with four whole pages describing it. The six hundred which follow demonstrate in enormous detail how the sisters' lives are entirely shaped by the Five Towns and other factors of which they are scarcely aware – by accumulated, sometimes tiny 'errors of destiny' in daily existence; even a broken tooth or an unwound watch. On the one hand, the novel communicates in this way an extraordinarily expansive, detailed vision of ordinary people in their ordinary quotidian lives – of the whole existence of the kind of person Bennett suggests in his Preface would 'pass unnoticed in a crowd' (p.22). *The Old Wives' Tale*, however, also establishes how completely even such vividly imagined individuals are the victims of environment, circumstance, and ultimately time.

E.M. Forster takes a more optimistic view of life in general, and of challenges particular to the Edwardian era. Like some of the authors discussed above, Forster shows in his early career a determination to reject constraints in family and social life left over from the Victorian period. In *A Room with a View* (1908), for example, he charts the experience of a heroine whose increasing openness to art, passion and vitality helps her achieve an individual freedom from conventionality and restraint. Personal relations remain a central concern throughout much of Forster's career, but in *Howards End* (1910) he also moves on to examine the kind of broader social issues which concerned Galsworthy, Wells and Bennett. Like these authors, Forster surveys an increasingly inequitable, disintegral society, darkened by the 'telegrams and anger' which rule the heartless business enterprise of the Wilcoxes, and menaced by the creeping 'rust' of cities which threaten to overwhelm older, more liberal values still surviving in the countryside. Nevertheless, unlike Forster's later *A Passage to India* (1924) – which sees no real solution to cultural conflicts between East and West generated by empire – *Howards End* still suggests redeeming possibilities for restoring wholeness to contemporary life, despite its fragmentation and class division. Throughout the novel, Forster summarises in the motto 'only connect' hopes for a spirit of liberal tolerance and understanding even among diverse social groups and factions. This possibility is illustrated in the relationship between Margaret Schlegel and Henry Wilcox, which suggests a chance for integration between the artistic, spiritual domain represented by the Schlegels and the soulless but pragmatic materialism of the Wilcoxes. Their marriage allows *Howards End* to conclude in a mood of qualified liberal optimism.

As Forster shows in *Howards End* – and Orwell confirms in *Coming up for Air* – liberal politics had a strong hold in the Edwardian period, especially in the countryside. With the collaboration of the recently formed Labour Party, the Liberals won in 1906 a sweeping electoral victory which allowed them to begin tackling some of the social problems of the age. Their programme of reforms, however – designed to create an embryonic version of the Welfare State – soon encountered resistance from the House of Lords, which rejected Lloyd George's reforming Budget in 1909. After several political crises, it became clear by December 1910 that the Liberals had the power to carry out their wishes, if necessary by abolishing the House of Lords. Significant for contemporary politics, the date of December 1910 has also acquired a particular resonance within literary history. Succinctly emphasising the shifting, unstable nature of the Edwardian period, Virginia Woolf famously remarked in her essay 'Mr. Bennett and Mrs. Brown' (1924), that 'in or about December, 1910, human character changed'. Her choice of date for something as significant and far-reaching as a change in human character is provocatively specific, and has been much discussed. Most commentators suggest that Woolf had in mind the exhibition of Post-Impressionist painting which her friend Roger Fry helped to organise in London in December 1910, challenging the Edwardians with revolutionary possibilities of style and form in art. It seems likely, however, that – among other factors to be considered in Chapter Two – contemporary political events also played a part in Woolf's choice of date. The Liberals' redirection of power away from the aristocracy represented in the House of Lords indicated a permanent alteration in the social and class divisions so central to British life, and so often a subject for novelists. Something of this kind of change is examined in 'Mr. Bennett and Mrs. Brown', which at one stage suggests that, for Woolf, the real 'Invasion of 1910' was made not by sinister German forces, but by her cook, rising from the lower depths of the Victorian kitchen, bursting into the previously forbidden domain of the living room to borrow a newspaper, confirming Woolf's view that 'all human relations have shifted'.[5]

Woolf's essay, however, is significant not only for its indication of profound change within the Edwardian period, but for her suggestion of what its consequences ought to have been for literature, and her evaluation of contemporary authors in terms of their responses to this changing age. Woolf criticises Arnold Bennett, John Galsworthy and H.G. Wells – 'the most prominent and successful novelists in the year 1910', as she calls them – for an incapacity to represent human nature in general, and a particular inability to deal with the new demands and shifting nature of their times. Her views have influenced later assessments of these authors substantially, and perhaps unfairly: as the above discussion suggested, Bennett, Wells and Galsworthy were often concerned very directly with the new materialism and other contemporary problems. Woolf, however, objected to their work not for any inattentiveness to contemporary society, but rather to the manner in which its attention was paid; even to a certain excess in it. Her criticism focuses on the kind of extended descriptive passage – mentioned earlier – which intrudes upon the account of the heroine's courtship in *Anna of the Five Towns*. Discussing Bennett's later novel *Hilda Lessways* (1911), Woolf suggests that such passages become a kind of permanent distraction from the heroine herself. In her view, Bennett's determination to 'describe . . . describe . . . describe', and his concern with 'telling us facts', place such 'enormous stress on the fabric of things' that he was never able to look truly or sympathetically 'at life . . . at human nature'.[6] In one way, of course, such criticism misses the point of Bennett's fiction, whose constant description of background and circumstance is not necessarily an evasion of human nature, but an attempt to document the forces which construct and shape it. Yet in another way, as Woolf suggests, so much objective, documentary description of environment and background also has negative effects on Bennett's novels – and to some extent on those of Wells and Galsworthy. It creates a kind of materialism in their novels at a level of style, making their work inadvertently complicit with the very aspects of contemporary life they set out to criticise. Concentration on environmental factors of which characters had 'never been conscious' diminishes attention to consciousness itself; to the life of the mind or spirit which might offer some untainted inner space beyond the reach of modern industrial, materialist society.

Similar criticisms of 'the most prominent and successful novelists in the year 1910' also appear in the comments of other contemporary writers. Like Woolf, D.H. Lawrence complained of John Galsworthy that his characters are 'only materially and socially conscious'. This is a consequence, he suggests, of Galsworthy's diversion of interest from 'the psychology of the free human individual into the psychology of the social being . . . too much aware of objective reality'[7] – a fault accentuated in Galsworthy's writing as the Forsyte series dragged on into the 1920s. By this time, as Chapter Two explains, Woolf, Lawrence and other authors had found means to avoid social being, objective reality, and the material world, concentrating instead on the more subjective, inward dimensions of character and presenting with new intimacy 'the psychology of the free human individual'. Steps in this direction, however, were also initiated in the Edwardian period itself by Henry James, Ford Madox Ford and Joseph Conrad. Significantly, all three were in some way outsiders to Britain – James was American by origin; Conrad a Pole who learned French before English; and Ford of German descent. Their relative independence from English society and literary conventions may have contributed to their readiness to reshape the novel and sometimes move beyond its immediate social concerns.

Like Woolf, Henry James criticised his contemporaries for a kind of materialism in style. He was also particularly concerned with a related inadequacy in their work as art – with the consequences of Wells's readiness to work as 'a journalist rather than an artist'. In James's view, such attitudes among contemporary authors led to sprawling novels rather than the precisely shaped, artistically ordered ones he sought. In discussing Bennett's *The Old Wives' Tale*, for example, James complained that

> The canvas is covered, ever so closely and vividly covered, by the exhibition of innumerable small facts and aspects . . . a monument exactly not to an idea, a pursued and captured meaning, or, in short, to anything whatever, but just simply of the quarried and gathered material it happens to contain, the stones and bricks and rubble and cement.[8]

For James, this quarried material – 'a slice of life' – could not of itself constitute a satisfactory novel: the 'inclusion and confusion' of reality should be further 'wrought and shaped' into significant form. This James considered achieved for his own work by the use of a 'structural centre', the kind of focusing figure created by his

> instinctive disposition . . . which consists in placing advantageously, placing right in the middle of the light, the most polished of possible mirrors of the subject.[9]

James illustrates this disposition with the 'unmistakeable example' of Lambert Strether in *The Ambassadors* (1903). The novel is 'wrought and shaped' by concentration around the perspective of Strether, an 'intense perceiver', as James calls him, of the complex web of social manners and relationships encountered during his delicate mission to Paris. Strether, however, is an American relatively innocent of European wiles and subtleties: although he is an intense perceiver, he is at first a limited, uninitiated one. The interest of *The Ambassadors* therefore centres not only, as James's metaphor might suggest, on what the mirror shows – on 'the subject' of the Parisian society Strether observes – but rather on the particular nature and gradually increasing sophistication of the mirror itself: on Strether's perception, mind, and reactions. These are communicated with unusual depth and intimacy by James's concentration of a whole novel around them. Along with other late works – such as *What Maisie Knew* (1897) – *The Ambassadors* thus moves the interest of the novel (rather as Impressionism had for recent painting) from what James calls 'the spreading field, the human scene' to 'the reflected field' of the mind which envisages it. This interest in what he describes as placing 'the centre of the subject in . . . consciousness' or 'courting . . . noiseless mental footsteps'[10] shows in James's writing an early form of the priorities which shape the work of some of the authors discussed in Chapter Two.

Ford and Conrad can be seen to share in this early development: each, like Henry James, accepted the label 'Impressionist' for his work. Ford was an admirer of James, and the best of his early fiction, *The Good Soldier*, traces like *The Ambassadors* the perplexities of an innocent American encountering the intricacies of European society. The naïvety of the American concerned – John Dowell, the narrator of the novel – particularly appears in his failure for much of his married life to notice his wife's infidelity with Edward Ashburnham. Dowell's later account of the various episodes of this affair is delivered as if he were talking to 'a silent listener' and 'in a very rambling way' (p.167) ruled by the fickleness of his memory. The complexity of the narrative which results is further increased by Dowell's variously plausible self-justifications, self-contradictions, understandable resentments and ignorance of the 'unconscious desires' (p.213) which often shape what he actually says. Such foibles make him an early but typical example of the unreliable narrators who often appear in the twentieth-century novel – one of its distinctive departures from Victorian fiction, whose omniscient authors reflect the outlook of a less uncertain age; perhaps corresponding to faith in an omniscient, omnipotent God. Unreliable figures such as Dowell require readers to examine the means through which a story is told, and the nature of the teller, as well as what is told. In this way Ford shares some of James's interest in moving the novel's attention away from the perceived world in order to examine in more detail the nature of perception and the psychology of the perceiver.

Henry James praised Conrad for finding, in novels such as *Lord Jim*, *Heart of Darkness*, *Chance* and *Under Western Eyes* (1911) a 'structural centre' of his own – the narrator Marlow, a figure within the fiction around whose perceptions the material of the novel could be structured. In one way, Marlow does function as James suggests. In another, however, Conrad's use of him also dramatises the ultimate impossibility of structuring or making complete sense of any experience, in life or the novel. Marlow is a figure of more limited, uncertain vision even than Strether, confessing in *Lord Jim* that he sees Jim at best hazily, as if through 'shifting rents in a thick fog' (p.63). Marlow, moreover, is rarely a direct observer himself, but pieces together his information in *Lord Jim* from many other – inevitably biased or limited – witnesses of Jim's story. Their various testimonies Marlow forms into the immense after-dinner monologue and later letter which make up most of the novel. Like Ford, with whom he collaborated in writing *The Inheritors* (1900) and *Romance* (1903), Conrad uses the device of a narrator addressing 'silent listeners'; structuring the story – 'a free and wandering tale' as he calls it in his Author's Note (p.7) – in a rambling way determined by the sequence of Marlow's recollections and assembled testimonies, rather than the order of the actual events of Jim's story.

As a result, *Lord Jim* itself takes the form of a shifting fog of various conflicting visions, voices, and recollections. Through this form, Conrad emphasises the impossibility of knowing reality with certainty, objectivity, or independence of relative, individual perceptions and versions of events. In Conrad's fiction – as in much contemporary philosophy – the old stable elephant of the Edwardians is disturbed not only by the erosion of faiths and values in the society round its feet, but by dissolution of secure means of knowing the world at all. 'For a time,' Marlow records in *Heart of Darkness*, 'I would feel I belonged still to a world of straightforward facts; but the feeling would not last long' (p.40). Straightforward facts vanish from *Lord Jim* as early as the first sentence – 'He was an inch, perhaps two, under six feet' – which suggests an observer uncertain even of Jim's physical stature. Later, Jim himself contemptuously dismisses facts: 'Facts! . . . as if facts could explain anything!' (p.27). Such scepticism about facts puts Conrad in direct opposition to Wells's assumptions about the true business of a novelist. Conrad is also set apart from the other 'prominent and successful novelists in the year 1910' by the extent to which he makes conflicting visions and uncertainties part of the form of the novel, rather than only part of its subject and theme. Conveniently published in 1900, and emphasising contemporary uncertainty in its structure as well as its story of failed imperial heroism, discussed earlier, Conrad's *Lord Jim* has a good claim to being the first truly modern novel in English. It is at any rate one of the first to demonstrate a possibility greatly

developed by fiction in later decades of the twentieth century –
that the novel could be radically altered in terms of structure and
style, rather than story alone, to take account of the challenges
and changed outlook of a new age.

Other aspects of the development of twentieth-century fiction
can also be seen as partly consequent upon the stresses of the
Edwardian age, and anticipated in the differences which
separated Ford, James, and Conrad from other novelists at the
time. An example of this appears in the dispute which arose
when Wells replied to James's criticism by suggesting that the
latter's finely detailed interest in individual consciousnesses –
such as Strether's in *The Ambassadors* – made his novels finicky in
their sensitivities and over-elaborate in language and style.
Wells's and James's differences help define a wider division in
contemporary and later views about the proper nature and
function of fiction. On the one hand, Wells supports the novel of
social concern and commitment – realistic in style; broad in
appeal; and on the whole traditional rather than innovative in
form and structure. James, on the other, favours interest in the
depths of individual mind and emotion, and in the novel as art –
sophisticated and sometimes challenging in style and form;
ready to depart if necessary from the realistic conventions of the
Victorian age. As the Introduction suggested, the conflict of
these sets of priorities was partly a new phenomenon in the
Edwardian era: the precedence of one or other set helps
distinguish various movements and periods recognisable in the
later development of twentieth-century fiction. Jamesian ideas
predominate in the modernist phase examined in the next
chapter. In the thirties and some of the next two decades, the
fifties especially, Wellsian preferences often reappear in various
ways. It is only in the closing years of the century that the
fracture James and Wells defined shows signs of beginning to
heal.

By the time James's dispute with Wells had reached its height
in 1914, contemporary events had brought the Edwardian era to
a decisive end – and had begun to contribute to the novel's
movement towards the kind of interests outlined by James and,
later, Virginia Woolf. It is significant that Woolf picks December
1910, and not August 1914, as the date on which 'human
character changed': her choice helps to confirm that the First

World War was neither the first nor the only factor in the changing character of the times. Nevertheless, however much the Boer War dented imperial confidence; however disturbingly the relative stability of the Victorian era dissolved away beneath the apparently solid surface of the Edwardian one, as Orwell suggests it was the end of July 1914, and the posters everywhere declaring war on Germany, which made the ghastly flux of modern life finally impossible to ignore. 'It was in 1915 the old world ended', D.H. Lawrence suggests in *Kangaroo* (1923) – a date also chosen by Compton Mackenzie, who saw in the introduction of conscription in that year a final blow to the old ideals of gentlemanliness and gallantry which had supposedly sustained the Empire. After the war, the prominent and successful novelists of 1910 – however seriously they had rebelled themselves against the conventions of Victorianism – seemed in retrospect conservatives; citizens of a vanished world, buried beneath the disasters of Flanders. Five months after the war ended, Virginia Woolf began to argue in her essay 'Modern Fiction' the case she extends in 'Mr. Bennett and Mrs. Brown' and enacts in her own writing throughout the twenties, as the next chapter shows – the need for a new novel, adjusted to the conditions and demands of a new age.

FURTHER READING

John Batchelor *The Edwardian Novelists*, London: Duckworth, 1982.

Jefferson Hunter *Edwardian Fiction*, Cambridge, Massachusetts: Harvard University Press, 1982.

Peter Keating *The Haunted Study: A social history of the English novel 1875–1914*, London: Secker and Warburg, 1989.

Anthea Trodd *A Reader's Guide to Edwardian Literature*, Hemel Hempstead: Harvester Wheatsheaf, 1991.

2 *A Myriad Impressions*

The Modernist Novel

'I will invent a new name for my books to supplant "novel"',
Virginia Woolf remarked in her diary in 1925, 'But what?
Elegy?'[1] The novel she was working on at the time, *To the
Lighthouse*, offers in several aspects, further considered throughout this chapter, a paradigm for ways in which the conventions
of Edwardian and earlier fiction were 'supplanted' during and
after the First World War – changes perhaps radical enough to
justify Woolf's wish for a new name for the novel. *To the
Lighthouse* does provide a kind of elegy both for the Edwardian
age and for its styles of fiction, differences between its three
sections illustrating how the end of one era encouraged new
vision in the literature of the next. Set in a bright summer before
the war, during the Ramsays' happy family holiday in the
Hebrides, the first section – 'The Window' – is full of cheerful
expectations for the future. It continues to share in the
conventions of many Edwardian and earlier novels, showing
lives developing towards a secure conclusion and an achieved
coherence in life and society. It ends with Mrs Ramsay's
successful dinner party – during which she hears of the
forthcoming marriage of her guests Paul and Minta – and with
her own marriage drawn back into tranquil harmony while her
bright, promising children sleep peacefully upstairs.

The second section, 'Time Passes', suggests how fragile and
ephemeral all this is. Covering the years of the First World War,
it emphasises the transience of emotions – including Paul and

Minta's – and of life itself. It shows the deaths of Mrs Ramsay's bright son Andrew, in the trenches; of her daughter Prue; and even of Mrs Ramsay herself. In the third section, 'The Lighthouse', the vestiges of the family and their friends return for another Hebridean holiday in the desolate years after the war. Significantly, the figure who replaces Mrs Ramsay as the centre of attention in this section, Lily Briscoe, seeks to create harmony and coherence not in social terms or in the life of the family, but through the form and stability of art, in her work as a painter. The novel ends when she successfully completes her painting and remarks, perhaps speaking for Woolf herself, 'I have had my vision' (p.237).

This conclusion and the novel's movement as a whole are typical of the tendency considered in this chapter – to despair of coherence in a materialist, chaotic social life, increasingly bereft of religious, moral or historical certainties, and to see art, vision and the depths of the individual spirit as the only refuge from this disorder. Several other novels published during or after the First World War, such as D.H. Lawrence's *The Rainbow* (1915), or James Joyce's *Ulysses* (1922), likewise end in satisfying *vision* of life, rather than the achievement of much coherence in the actual lives of the characters themselves. This contrasts clearly with the Edwardian fiction discussed in Chapter One. However much novelists such as H.G. Wells or E.M. Forster were disturbed by the problems of their age, they still considered that these difficulties could be resolved by more enlightened ideas or better social organisation, and that, meanwhile, they could be highlighted in novels of fairly conventional realist style. After the war, as T.S. Eliot suggested in 1923, the novel as it had hitherto existed seemed 'a form which will no longer serve'. It was therefore necessary for fiction to find what Eliot calls new ways 'of controlling, of ordering, of giving a shape and a significance to the immense panorama of futility and anarchy which is contemporary history'.[2] As Eliot recommended, Virginia Woolf and her contemporaries sought in new forms of art – rather than in new social ideas – compensation for the apparent chaos of contemporary history; finding new ways of writing in which the individual could still be seen as significant and whole, the self and soul intact, despite the pressure of the age. It is this change in forms of writing and the desirability of new vision in the novel which Woolf advocates in the essays mentioned in Chapter One, 'Modern Fiction' (1919) and 'Mr. Bennett and Mrs. Brown' (1924). Novelists sharing this determination to break with the conventions of the past, to be deliberately modern, have come to be labelled by critics as 'modernists'.

Modernist writing can be seen as the major initiative for change and development in twentieth-century fiction, establishing a new vision and a new set of strategies for the novel, and is therefore worth considering in detail. In the fiction of the modernist writers examined in this chapter – principally D.H. Lawrence, May Sinclair, Dorothy Richardson, James Joyce, Wyndham Lewis and Virginia Woolf herself – departures from convention can be considered in three separate areas. New, sometimes self-conscious interest in art and artist-figures such as Lily Briscoe in *To the Lighthouse* will be considered later, as will new means of structuring the novel. What is often considered the central interest and achievement of modernist fiction is discussed first. This was identified in its early stages in Chapter One in the fiction of Henry James, Joseph Conrad and Ford Madox Ford – each of whose work shows an embryonic form of modernism's distinctive, subjective concentration on 'the psychology of the free human individual', as D.H. Lawrence puts it, rather than on the 'objective reality' he and other modernists felt limited the work of many of the Edwardians.

To the Lighthouse once again illustrates the nature of this new emphasis and some of the reasons for it. The main interest of Mr Ramsay's philosophy is defined as 'Subject and object and the nature of reality' (p.28): this is also a central concern of the novel itself, its three sections demonstrating and exploring the different possibilities and values of subjective and objective vision. The second section, 'Time Passes', is concerned not only with war and death but with the domain of objects and things independent of consciousness – the natural world of stones, stars, dust and the wind which surrounds the family's holiday home during the long years of their absence. For many nineteenth-century writers – for Romantic poets, fleeing the new urbanisation of the Industrial Revolution; for novelists as late as Thomas Hardy in the 1890s, or even E.M. Forster in *Howards End* (1910) – this kind of natural, pastoral world offered a refuge from social pressure, and sometimes a kind of extension or reflection of the emotions of the self. For Woolf, however, this no longer seems viable. The wind frets and gnaws destructively at the family's house, and a corrupted natural world – the sea darkly stained by the naval actions of the First World War – offers no consoling reflection of the self. Instead, 'it was difficult', the novel records,

> to continue, as one walked by the sea, to marvel how beauty outside mirrored beauty within.
>
> Did Nature supplement what man advanced? Did she complete what he began? With equal complacence she saw his misery, condoned his meanness, and acquiesced in his torture . . . the mirror was broken. (p.153)

Lack of coherence or beauty outside forced the writer to seek it within: like most of the modernists, it is not external but inner nature that Woolf favours. As an alternative to the 'broken mirror' of external reality, she suggests that only 'in those mirrors, the minds of men . . . dreams persisted . . . good triumphs, happiness prevails, order rules' (pp.150–1). It is this kind of mirror that Woolf employs in the first and third sections of *To the Lighthouse*. Her methods for recording its polished perceptions differ from those of James, Conrad or Ford and can be illustrated in the following passage, showing Mrs Ramsay at her triumphal dinner party towards the end of 'The Window':

> Just now (but this cannot last, she thought, dissociating herself from the moment while they were all talking about boots) just now she had reached security; she hovered like a hawk suspended; like a flag floated in an element of joy which filled every nerve of her body fully and sweetly, not noisily, solemnly rather, for it arose, she thought, looking at them all eating there, from husband and children and friends; all of which rising in this profound stillness (she was helping William Bankes to one very small piece more and peered into the depths of the earthenware pot) seemed now for no special reason to stay there like a smoke, like a fume rising upwards, holding them safe together. Nothing need be said; nothing could be said. (pp.120–1)

The passage follows and imitates in its rhythm the expanding associations in Mrs Ramsay's thoughts as they swirl away from the immediate scene, dissociating themselves from a banal external reality, domain of boots and second helpings, which is relegated to the relative insignificance of parentheses. While Ford and Conrad record the voice of a narrator supposedly addressing other silent listeners, passages like the one above show Woolf following a character silently, inwardly addressing herself, establishing a private, inner world from which 'Nothing need be said; nothing could be said' by way of connection with the public one around her. Not only the first and third sections of *To the Lighthouse*, but much of Woolf's *Mrs Dalloway* (1925) and *The Waves* (1931) represent in this way the unspoken, innermost thoughts, the interior monologue of her characters.

Such writing fulfils Woolf's demand in 'Modern Fiction' that the novel should

> Look within and . . . examine . . . an ordinary mind on an ordinary day. The mind receives a myriad impressions . . . Is it not the task of the novelist to convey this varying, this unknown and uncircum- scribed spirit . . . with as little mixture of the alien and external as possible? . . . to reveal the flickerings of that innermost flame which flashes its messages through the brain.[3]

By the time Woolf wrote *To the Lighthouse* – even by the time she made her suggestion in 'Modern Fiction' – several other novelists had already evolved their own tactics for avoiding 'the alien and external' in favour of transcribing the inner spirit. One of these is D.H. Lawrence, whose interest in 'the psychology of the free human individual' is sometimes considered to have been particularly motivated by a new factor in the thinking of his time – the work of Sigmund Freud, first translated into English in 1909. In a draft, unpublished form of 'Mr. Bennett and Mrs. Brown', Woolf adds to the possible motives – outlined in Chapter One – for her choice of December 1910 as the date on which 'human character changed' by straightforwardly suggest- ing it did so for 'scientific reasons' such as the influence of Freud.[4] This influence might be identified at many points in the work of modernist authors – in their general readiness to 'look within'; or in their showing the self sometimes shaped by forces beyond immediate consciousness. In Lawrence's case, in particular, Paul Morel's problems in *Sons and Lovers* (1913) might be seen as the result of an Oedipus complex of the kind identified by Freud. Freud's influence might also be traced in Lawrence's rejection of 'the old stable *ego*' of character, or in his fiction's general interest in forces and passions belonging to what it calls 'another centre of consciousness', one 'beyond thought'.

Lawrence, however, considered Freud's ideas no more than 'partly true',[5] and shows throughout his fiction other motives for looking within, away from an external reality made uncongenial in some of the same ways Woolf suggests in *To the Lighthouse*. *Sons and Lovers* shows the green, natural landscape of Nottingham vanishing beneath the black collieries and their greying wastes: the menace to the 'free human individual' of the advancing industrialism and materialism of the modern world is investigated in greater detail in Lawrence's best novels, *The Rainbow* and *Women in Love* (1921). The former charts the experience of the Brangwen family in the later nineteenth century, following disruption of the long-standing stability of their rural life and agricultural work. The earlier Brangwens 'knew the intercourse between heaven and earth . . . the pulse and body of the soil' (p.8) but in the 1840s their organic intimacy with nature is interrupted, their land literally sliced across by the canal – described as 'the cut' (p.248) – and the railways introduced by the Industrial Revolution. Succeeding genera-tions inhabit a more and more complicated world, its once-rural landscape increasingly dominated by 'the great colliery . . . the great machine which has taken us all captives' (p.350). Follow-ing a later generation of Brangwens, *Women in Love* explores a fragmentary society, presided over by 'the industrial magnate' (p.237), Gerald. Convinced of 'the pure instrumentality of mankind' and 'the pure machine-principle', his reform of the coal mines ensures

> the substitution of the mechanical principle for the organic . . . pure organic disintegration and pure mechanical organisation . . .
>
> The miners were reduced to mere mechanical instruments.
>
> (pp.250, 256, 259, 260)

Materialism and mechanisation of this kind – 'the cruelty of iron and the smoke of coal, and the endless, endless greed that drove it all' – creates what Lawrence calls in *Lady Chatterley's*

Lover (1928) 'the utter, soulless ugliness of the coal-and-iron Midlands' (pp.149, 14). This landscape in Lawrence's fiction often resembles Arnold Bennett's in his novels of the Five Towns, a similarity especially marked in *The Lost Girl* (1920). This soulless landscape and the deadened, mechanical nature of its inhabitants Lawrence nevertheless sees as redeemable – at least in *The Rainbow* – by the kind of full, balanced relationship between the sexes which is represented by the symbol of the rainbow itself. In the novel's optimistic, almost mystic, conclusion, a vision of its balanced, over-arching shape suggests the possibility of restoring and reintegrating the whole squalid, industrialised society which stands beneath. *Women in Love, The Lost Girl* and *Lady Chatterley's Lover* are more pessimistic, showing only certain privileged or fortunate couples able to escape the dispiriting effects of what Lawrence calls 'the modern, industrial and financial world' (*Lady Chatterley's Lover*, p.114).

Typically of modernist writers, however, it is through reshaping the form of the novel itself that Lawrence tries to resist this world's materialism, mechanisation and denial of a full, integrated existence for the self. Acknowledging the disappearance from the modern world – and the modern novel – of 'the old stable *ego*', Lawrence suggests that 'a deeper sense than any we've been used to exercise' could still sustain for fiction a continuing sense of complete, coherent individuality. In one way, his fiction establishes this deeper sense simply by means of the increased extent to which it directs readers' attention upon subjective, inner feelings. Often, description of events or action in Lawrence's novels – sometimes single lines of conversation – are followed by paragraphs or even pages reporting his characters' thoughts and emotions. This communicates more fully than in much conventional fiction the ebb and flow, wonder and disillusion of relationships and their effect on the individual.

Lawrence, however, presents this inner experience not only by report, but often by moving towards transcription of characters' inner thoughts themselves. Ursula Brangwen's deepening reflections in *Women in Love* illustrate his means of doing so:

> And the next step was over the border into death. So it was
> then! . . .
>   It was a decision. It was not a question of taking one's life – she
> would *never* kill herself, that was repulsive and violent. It was a
> question of *knowing* the next step. And the next step led into the
> space of death. Did it? – or was there – ?
>   Her thoughts drifted into unconsciousness. (pp.214–15)

Inverted commas, 'she thought' or 'she said to herself' are
missing, but the rhetorical questions, exclamations and italicised
emphases of certain words suggest that – until the authorial
report of the last sentence – the drifting thoughts in this passage
belong to Ursula rather than the novelist. The transcription of
these thoughts is nevertheless not exact – Ursula would talk of
herself as 'I', not 'she' – but obviously mediated and arranged by
the author. Neither direct speech nor the kind of indirect speech
very often used by Woolf ('this cannot last, she thought'; 'it
arose, she thought'), this means of approximating to a character's
inner voice is usually known as Free Indirect Style. It is by no
means Lawrence's invention. It is used by Henry James to help
keep his narrative in *The Ambassadors* (1903) focused around the
perception of Strether, and in the nineteenth century, extensively, by Jane Austen and Charles Dickens, for example. The
extent of Lawrence's reliance on it, however – like Woolf's on
indirect speech (sometimes also Free Indirect) – is new, and
marks a particular stage in novelists' extension, in the early
twentieth century, of techniques employed to look within the
mind.

   This is also apparent in the later work of Ford Madox Ford,
which moves beyond the supposedly spoken monologue of *The
Good Soldier* (1915) to record the inner musing of Ford's hero
Christopher Tietjens and other figures in his *Parade's End*
tetralogy (1924–8). Questions, self-contradictions, and abbreviated sentences interrupted by pauses imitate some of the
style, rhythm and hesitations of thought, showing Ford, like
Lawrence, using a form of Free Indirect Style. Such tactics are
particularly appropriately employed in *Parade's End*, one of the
most substantial English treatments of the First World War –
both its violent action in the trenches and its disturbing effects
within domestic society. The fragmented, disjointed language

Ford uses to represent the thought of his characters, Tietjens particularly, strongly communicates the stresses of the war and their pressures within the mind of the individual.

Lawrence's fiction seeks within its characters' minds spaces still free from the forces of the modern industrial and financial world. Other, comparable, motives for looking within can be seen to arise from what Henry James identified in 1899 as one of the most significant changes in the life of his time – 'the revolution taking place in the position and outlook of women'.[6] His prediction that new features and styles in fiction would result was fulfilled in several ways, not all of them confined to the work of women writers. For example, the widespread appearance of the *femme fatale* in early twentieth-century novels – in the work of Wyndham Lewis, Ford Madox Ford, Aldous Huxley and others – may be a figuration of male anxieties about women's new assertions of freedom and rejection of conventional social roles during the suffragette period. 'The woman question', suffragism, and the general issue of female independence are also treated more substantially and sympathetically in fiction in the early twentieth century. They are central concerns in Elizabeth Robins's *The Convert* (1907) and H.G. Wells's *Ann Veronica* (1909), for example. They are also important issues in Dorothy Richardson's *Pilgrimage* (1915-67), whose heroine Miriam Henderson tries with varying success to establish her freedom from contemporary social constraints. In the thirteen volumes of *Pilgrimage*, Richardson is able to trace in detail Miriam's struggle for financial independence – first as a schoolteacher in Germany and London, then an office-worker – as well as her assertions of new freedoms such as smoking in public or cycling alone. Occasionally, *Pilgrimage* simply records Miriam's bitter resentment of a world dominated by men, whom she finds 'simply paltry and silly – all of them'. She concludes that 'all the men in the world, and their God, ought to apologise to women' (II, p.206; I, p.459).

Women's changed perception of contemporary society and their roles within it affected not only the subject and ideas of fiction, but also its form and style. Part of Miriam Henderson's resentment of men is that literature is dominated by 'some mannish cleverness that was only half right' (II, p.131).

Richardson herself likewise explains that she sought 'a feminine equivalent of the current masculine realism' – particularly wishing to avoid, like Virginia Woolf, the manner of Arnold Bennett.[7] This interest in developing a specifically feminine form of writing coincided in some ways with the contemporary urge to 'look within' and 'examine the mind'. Writing in 1929, Virginia Woolf suggested that feminine independence required what the title of her study calls 'A Room of One's Own'. In a male-dominated society, one of the few places that such a 'room' could be discovered was in the private space of the individual mind, in a 'splitting off of consciousness', as Woolf calls it, from external reality.[8] Women writers may therefore have been particularly attracted to techniques which could allow the novel to look within and inhabit this private space.

They may also have been particularly equipped to move through the various stages necessary in the full development of such techniques. However promising the inner spaces of the mind may have seemed, it was hard for women to ignore the extent to which in a male-dominated world they continued to be envisaged objectively – even as objects – in terms of outward appearance and not subjective inner nature. Subject and object and the nature of reality, in other words, may have been central concerns not just in Mr Ramsay's philosophy, nor only for Woolf herself, but for contemporary women writers more generally. A particularly sharp, dual awareness of the self as both object and subject – though problematic in life – may nevertheless have facilitated the development of certain styles in fiction. This can be seen in the following passage from an early volume of *Pilgrimage*:

> She [Miriam] was surprised now at her familiarity with the detail of the room . . . that idea of visiting places in dreams. It was something more than that . . . all the real part of your life has a real dream in it; some of the real dream part of you coming true. You know in advance when you are really following your life. These things are familiar because reality is here. Coming events cast *light*. It is like dropping everything and walking backwards to something you know is there. However far you go out, you come back . . . I am back now where I was before I began trying to do things like other

people. I left home to get here. None of these things can touch me here. (II, p.13)

The passage moves from the apparently distanced view of Miriam as 'she' into the more intimate, indeterminate 'you', partly a transcription of Miriam's inner voice. A more crucial step from objective to subjective is taken in the last sentence, which moves into an 'I' form, in the present tense. This seems to transcribe Miriam's thoughts directly, in the form in which they occur to her, apparently independent even of the authorial mediation of Free Indirect Style. Such sections of apparently direct recording of thought expand in frequency and scale as the novel-sequence progresses, regularly conveying in their fragmented phrases Miriam's fleeting perceptions and wandering, associative impressions:

> I *must* have been through there; it's the park. I don't remember. It isn't. It's waiting. One day I will go through. Les yeux gris, vont au paradis. Going along, along, the twilight hides your shabby clothes . . . Everything's here, any bit of anything, clear in your brain; you can look at it. What a terrific thing a person is, bigger than anything . . . Hallo, old Euston Road, beloved of my soul, my own country, my native heath. (II, p.256)

Free from authorial comment, conveying Miriam's mind 'rushing on by itself' (I, p.268), such passages mark the first extensive appearance in English of one of the most distinctive and celebrated features of modernist fiction: the style which came to be known as 'stream of consciousness'. The phrase was first used to describe 'subjective life' by Henry James's brother, the philosopher William James, then was borrowed by May Sinclair. In a contemporary review, she describes an early volume of *Pilgrimage* as having

> no drama, no situation, no set scene. Nothing happens. It is just life going on and on. It is Miriam Henderson's stream of consciousness going on and on.[9]

Some of May Sinclair's own fiction is close to Dorothy Richardson's in subject and style. *Mary Olivier* (1919) follows like *Pilgrimage* a heroine struggling with roles and assumptions forced upon her by contemporary society. Tracing these struggles from her early childhood until she achieves a position of relative acquiescence and stability within society, *Mary Olivier* remains in some ways close to the kind of traditional *Bildungs-roman* mentioned in Chapter One. Sinclair's writing, however, also shows a modernist readiness – though less regularly employed than Richardson's – to move through Free Indirect Style and towards a form of stream of consciousness, recording, as *Mary Olivier* puts it, how 'your thoughts go on inside you' (p.99).

Critics have not always recognised the achievement of women writers – principally Woolf, Richardson and Sinclair – in evolving modernist techniques for looking within the mind, and it is only recently that there has been much recognition of the particular significance of Dorothy Richardson's role in this development. James Joyce, on the other hand, has always been praised as the master of the stream-of-consciousness style; almost too exclusively, as this can obscure his employment – in reflecting the minds of his protagonists in *Ulysses* – not only of stream of consciousness but of a wide range of the devices discussed above. His use of them develops throughout his earlier fiction. *Stephen Hero* – a prototype for *A Portrait of the Artist as a Young Man* which Joyce began in 1904 – is relatively conventional in style. When it does include attention to the inner life of its protagonist, this is mostly in the form of the author's report or description of his thoughts. Reworking this material into *A Portrait of the Artist as a Young Man* (1916), Joyce achieves a closer, Jamesian focus around and within Stephen's language and consciousness, often by means of Free Indirect Style. When Stephen reappears in the early chapters of *Ulysses*, Joyce presents his thoughts in the abbreviated, almost telegram-matic form often used in Richardson's writing – 'Come. I thirst. Clouding over. No black clouds anywhere, are there? Thunder-storm' (p.63). This form of stream of consciousness, however, is not uniformly sustained throughout *Ulysses*. For example, readers are introduced as follows to Joyce's main character Leopold Bloom, the Jewish advertising man whose experience during a Dublin day forms the substance of the novel:

> Mr Leopold Bloom ate with relish the inner organs of beasts and fowls . . .

Kidneys were in his mind as he moved about the kitchen softly, righting her breakfast things on the humpy tray. Gelid light and air were in the kitchen but out of doors gentle summer morning everywhere. Made him feel a bit peckish.

The coals were reddening.

Another slice of bread and butter: three, four: right. She didn't like her plate full. Right. He turned from the tray, lifted the kettle off the hob and set it sideways on the fire. It sat there, dull and squat, its spout stuck out. Cup of tea soon. Good. Mouth dry. (p.65)

Within a few lines of text, Joyce alternates between, on the one hand, the apparently objective authorial description of 'Mr Leopold Bloom ate with relish' or 'He turned from the tray' and, on the other, various means for registering inner thought – authorial report ('Kidneys were in his mind'), Free Indirect Style ('Made him feel a bit peckish') and stream of consciousness ('Cup of tea soon. Good. Mouth dry'). If as one critic suggests 'Joyce rewrote for the modern novel generally the definition of a man', it is partly as a result of the variety in technique and insight that such passages illustrate. They also show Joyce fulfilling his own ambition to create a 'complete all-round character'.[10] Especially in the first half of *Ulysses*, Bloom is constantly shown *from* all round; from inside as well as out; from a variety of points of view which range from the objective to the subjective.

As well as rewriting for the novel the definition of a man, *Ulysses* also fulfilled some of the conditions contemporary women writers thought necessary for the fictional representation of women. Joyce is one of the authors Dorothy Richardson praised for his creation of what she calls 'feminine prose . . . unpunctuated, moving from point to point without formal obstructions'.[11] Significantly, this unpunctuated prose is used in *Ulysses* to represent not Bloom's mind, but the private thoughts of his wife Molly, stirred into half-wakefulness when he returns home at the end of his epic Dublin day. She finds herself

thinking of so many things he didnt know of Mulvey and Mr Stanhope and Hester and father and old captain Groves and the sailors playing all birds fly and I say stoop and washing up dishes they called it on the pier . . . O and the sea the sea crimson sometimes like fire and the glorious sunsets and the figtrees in the Alameda gardens yes and all the queer little streets and the pink and blue and yellow houses and the rosegardens and the jessamine and the geraniums and cactuses and Gibraltar as a girl where I was a Flower of the mountain yes . . . (pp.932–3)

Joyce records this mingling flood of thought and memory for around sixty pages at the end of *Ulysses*. More genuinely a *stream* of consciousness than Bloom or Stephen's more fragmentary thoughts, Molly's myriad impressions of past and present – consummating the modernist novel's desire to 'look within and examine the mind' – are usually held to reach closer to the innermost flame of consciousness than any other fiction in the twentieth century. Along with its flexibility in ranging across a variety of the styles discussed above, this helps to make *Ulysses* what the critic Hugh Kenner calls 'the decisive English-language book of the century',[12] and Joyce himself the most admired and influential of twentieth-century novelists in English.

Joyce, however, rewrote for modern literature the definition not only of a man, or a woman, but of the novel itself, and his work also helps introduce the second main area of modernist innovation specified at the start of this chapter. *Ulysses* is revolutionary not only in style – in the extent and manner of its registration of inner consciousness – but in its overall means of structuring fiction. Most obviously, Joyce abandons the convention of following characters over an extended period of time – often, as in the *Bildungsroman*, of tracing their lives from birth to maturity. Like several other modernist novels (Virginia Woolf's *Mrs Dalloway*, for example), *Ulysses* largely renounces extended character history in favour of confinement, more or less as Woolf recommended, to 'an ordinary mind on an ordinary day' – the single day of Bloom's experience and mental life in Dublin on l6 June 1904. One reason for this new abbreviation in the time-span of fiction is suggested early in *Ulysses* when Stephen Dedalus describes history as 'a nightmare from which I am trying to awake' (p.42). For the Victorians and many of the Edwardians the onward flow of history and the life in time seemed sufficiently coherent and progressive to provide a valid structuring basis for the novel. Much fiction at this time, not only the *Bildungsroman*, follows relatively straightforward chronological progress from confusion and disequilibrium towards a point of satisfactory stability for individual and society. Especially after the First World War, the modernists found in history and the passage of time nightmare incoherence rather than developing order; a 'futility and anarchy', as Eliot puts it, which disposed them to consider that the structuring and ordering of fiction also needed to be changed.

To the Lighthouse is once again useful in clarifying the sources and consequences of this need. As discussed earlier, in its short, sharp, middle section the novel shows death and decay in the years of the First World War intruding between the Edwardian serenity of the first section and the desolate post-war summer treated in the third. In this way, *To the Lighthouse* shares the conclusion Richard Aldington reaches in one of the best and most bitter novels concerned with the First World War, *Death of a Hero* (1929). In assessing the 'long, unendurable nightmare' of the war (p.221) – and the hypocrisy and social malaise which he sees as part of its cause and result – Aldington remarks that the war left 'adult lives . . . cut sharply into three sections – pre-war, war, and post-war' (p.199). It is this kind of sectioning of contemporary experience which the three-part structure of *To the Lighthouse* reflects within the form of the novel. Woolf herself later talked of how the war 'cut into' contemporary life, seeming 'like a chasm in a smooth road'. D.H. Lawrence similarly considered it had left 'no smooth road' into the future.[13] For each of these writers, the war came as an interruption in the progress of history still sharper and deeper than the 'cut' of the Industrial Revolution had seemed in the lives, three-quarters of a century earlier, which Lawrence traces in *The Rainbow*. This sense of cut or chasm finally eradicated vestiges of the 'feeling of continuity' which George Orwell (in the passage quoted at the start of Chapter One) showed still strongly surviving in the Edwardian period.

The resulting sense of curtailment and fragmentation in the progress of history figures not only in Woolf's and Joyce's fiction, but in the work of other authors at the time, Lawrence's included. It helps account for the differences in structure between the two parts of what Lawrence originally conceived as a single project, 'The Sisters' – *The Rainbow*, largely written before the war, and *Women in Love*, completed during and after it. *The Rainbow* remains close to the kind of family saga form still used in the early twentieth century by John Galsworthy, showing similar patterns of experience evolving more or less continuously and coherently in successive generations of Brangwens in the nineteenth century. *Women in Love* is more fragmentary, often lacking clear sequential relations between chapters. Sometimes this makes the novel seem almost like a collection of short stories about characters' moods and individual experiences, rather than a sustained account of progress in their lives.

One of these characters, Gudrun, expresses a further aspect of modernist uncertainty about progress and the life in time when at the end of *Women in Love* she reflects on

> the mechanical succession of day following day . . . the terrible bondage of this tick-tack of time, this twitching of the hands of the clock, this eternal repetition of hours and days . . .
> The eternal, mechanical, monotonous clock-face of time.
>
> (pp.522–3)

Her anxieties are more specifically connected to the clock, and even to time itself, than to the wider uncertainties of contemporary history mentioned above. These feelings are also significantly connected to her lover Gerald, whom she sees as clock-like himself – made up of 'a million wheels and cogs and axles', adding to her horror of

> the wheels within wheels of people, it makes one's head tick like a clock, with a very madness of dead mechanical monotony and meaninglessness. (pp.525, 522)

By the end of the novel Gerald has become a victim of the very processes of mechanisation he initiated himself; reduced in Gudrun's vision to the same numb, mechanised state as the workers he controls. His condition exemplifies wider consequences of changes in late nineteenth-century working life – and the life in time – which are illustrated intermittently throughout *The Rainbow* and *Women in Love*. In the early stages of *The Rainbow*, the Brangwens' agricultural life and labour is as much cyclic as progressive, their experience measured by the eternal swing of the seasons and the sun's circling in the sky. This kind of life was destroyed by the Industrial Revolution, after which the railways' need for exact timetables, and factories' for co-ordinated shifts of workers, ensured that time grew increasingly systematised. It was eventually institutionalised in 1884 in the national – and international – standard of Greenwich Mean Time, which came to rule public and private life with increasing force. 'Clocking in' for factory work, and its organisation around principles of 'scientific management' based on 'time and motion' studies, had grown to be the norm by the early twentieth century – a new systematisation of working life specifically reflected in the 'Industrial Magnate' chapter of *Women in Love*. Gerald reorganises his mines to ensure that

> Everything was run on the most accurate and delicate scientific method . . . a new order, strict, terrible, inhuman . . . a great and perfect system that subjected life to pure mathematical principles.
> (pp.259–60)

General uneasiness with new systematisations of this kind – new bondages to the tick-tack of time in the modern industrial and financial world – helps explain a resentment of the clock which figures not only in Gudrun's feelings for Gerald in *Women in Love*, but throughout modernist fiction, Virginia Woolf's especially. Bernard, in *The Waves*, fears 'the stare of clocks' (p.25). *Mrs Dalloway* shows the clocks of Harley Street shredding and slicing, nibbling and diminishing its heroine's June day. Woolf's central character in *Orlando* (1928) suggests that 'it is a great shock to the nervous system, hearing a clock strike' (p.216). This kind of nervous response to the clock helps account for another aspect of the structure of modernist fiction, which not only concentrates its narrative within single days, but often radically departs from serial, chronological order within them. 'Life is not a series . . . symmetrically arranged', Woolf suggests in 'Modern Fiction', recording in her diary her determination to escape from 'this appalling narrative business of the realist: getting on from lunch to dinner'. Seeing this as 'false, unreal, merely conventional', she states instead her wish to 'read Proust' and 'go backwards and forwards'.[14] Like Marcel Proust's, Woolf's narratives do go backwards and forwards, departing from serial order by following the recollection of past events prompted for her characters by their experience of present ones. In this way, modernist concentration within the experience of single days does not altogether omit the broad acquaintance with characters' lives offered by earlier fiction: rather, it changes the manner in which it is made. *Orlando* suggests that 'memory is the seamstress, and a capricious one at that' (p.55): both Woolf and Joyce use it, still more fully than the narratives of Ford or Conrad discussed in Chapter One, to stitch into the fabric of present life and consciousness a range of recollected experiences – Bloom's memory of his father's death, for example; of his earlier life with Molly; the death of their son Rudi and so on. Lily Briscoe finds in the third section of *To the Lighthouse* that in memory she can rejoin Mrs Ramsay, happy on the beach before the war, 'as if a door had opened, and one went in and stood gazing silently about' in the past (p.195). At the end of *Ulysses*, Molly likewise passes through the door of memory, into a vision of recollected times, independent of the exigencies of the present.

Through such tactics, modernist fiction could partly escape the new bondage of the clock and the nightmare of contemporary history. Just as modernist authors turned away from the increasing pressures of social reality to the private inner space of consciousness, so they also moved into an inner dimension of memory; into what *Orlando* calls 'time in the mind' rather than 'time on the clock' (p.69). Resentment of the latter's increasing systematisation of life might also be seen figured in Joseph Conrad's *The Secret Agent* (1907), which concerns a plot to blow up the new universal clock at Greenwich. In this as in other areas, however, modernist fiction negotiates with the new stresses of modern life not through suggesting social or political action, but in aesthetic terms – certainly not, even in *The Secret Agent*, by advocating any actual plot against Greenwich, but by developing fictional structures and strategies which could diffuse, evade or assimilate Mean Time's new constraints upon contemporary life.

As discussed earlier, this kind of reliance on art and the aesthetic in modernist fiction is often re-emphasised in the views of its characters – Lily Briscoe remarking in *To the Lighthouse*, for example, that her painter's equipment is 'the one dependable thing in a world of strife, ruin, chaos' (p.170). This comment and others Lily makes throughout the novel help indicate the third principal area of modernism's new interests: its concern not only – like Henry James's fiction, or some of the Edwardian *Bildungsromans* discussed in Chapter One – with the nature of art in general, but also, self-consciously, with its own forms and styles. Lily provides a commentary in *To the Lighthouse* not just on her own work as an artist, but also by implication on the methods and structure of the novel in which she appears. Problems in her painting, such as 'how to connect this mass on the right hand with that on the left' and her solution for them – 'a line there, in the centre' (pp.62, 237) – are similar to Woolf's in shaping the tripartite structure of *To the Lighthouse* itself. James Joyce uses lengthy discussions of art similarly in *A Portrait of the Artist as a Young Man*, partly to examine and elucidate aesthetic views of his own, and Wyndham Lewis employs the artist-hero of his first published novel, *Tarr* (1918), as a mouthpiece for his own ideas about art and writing.

Tarr believes 'anything living, quick and changing is bad art always'; that 'good art must have no inside'; and that 'the soft inside of life . . . movement and consciousness' should be rigorously excluded from it (p.312). Such views made Lewis a natural adversary of modernism's determination to look within, and of the stream-of-consciousness form: he is an intriguing example of a highly innovative writer with a set of priorities almost opposite to those of the other modernists. He went on to develop further a case against Joyce, Woolf, and broader aspects of the life of his times in critical studies of contemporary culture such as *Men without Art* (1934) and *Time and Western Man* (1927); the latter locating in the work of Bergson, Einstein and other recent thinkers the origins of the modernist preference for 'time in the mind'. Ideas Tarr expresses continue to inform not only Lewis's criticism in the twenties, but much of his later fiction. Like *Tarr*, this often avoids attention to inner consciousness in favour of external observation and description. *The Apes of God* (1930) at times follows rigorously the 'external method' Lewis further discusses in *Men without Art*, using meticulous observation of physical gesture and speech to create a devastating satire of the community of leisured, pretentious artists in London in the twenties.

As *To the Lighthouse* and *Tarr* show, a self-conscious interest in the methods of fiction can be explored figuratively through the analogous activities and ideas of painters. Such self-consciousness, however, naturally moves beyond this analogy and comes to rest on the medium of fiction itself, language – an object of sometimes anxious attention throughout modernist writing. Lily Briscoe worries about the 'little words that broke up the thought and dismembered it' (p.202); Ursula in *Women in Love* that 'words themselves do not convey meaning' (p.209); while Miriam Henderson, in *Pilgrimage*, suggests that 'language is the only way of expressing anything and it dims everything' (II, p.99). Words may have seemed particularly dim or limiting to the modernists for a number of reasons. However successfully realised in the new stream-of-consciousness technique, modernism's urge to look within, if taken any further, ultimately encountered a limit – ordinary language's incapacity to represent movements of mind beyond conscious thinking. In *Ulysses*, Joyce leaves both Bloom and Molly at the point when each presumably falls asleep; similarly, in the passage quoted earlier from *Women in Love*, Lawrence ceases to record Ursula's thoughts when they 'drifted into unconsciousness'. Lawrence, however, has often been criticised for passages elsewhere in his fiction which attempt to go beyond this limit, stretching language towards the lurid in trying to represent the darkness and ecstasy of passions beyond thought. Such feelings are communicated more effectively by the many symbolic episodes in Lawrence's novels – and elsewhere in modernist fiction – which find scenes or objects that can figure or suggest the shapes of the unconscious or unsayable.

Shared by many modernist authors, the experience of exile further enforced awareness of the limitation of language, and of the particularity and arbitrariness of any individual form of it. For James Joyce, such doubts began even before he left Ireland, in ways indicated by Stephen Dedalus in *A Portrait of the Artist as a Young Man*. An encounter with an English priest suggests to him that, by comparison, he is not fully a native speaker of his own language: he discovers that English is both 'so familiar and so foreign' and that his 'soul frets in the shadow of his language' (p.189).

Such fretting contributes to the concern and fascination with words, sometimes almost independent of their meaning, recorded at several stages of *A Portrait of the Artist as a Young Man*. Initiated himself into several languages, familiar or foreign, during a lifetime spent mostly in Trieste, Zurich and Paris rather than Dublin, Joyce greatly extends this sort of interest in *Ulysses*. Parody shapes *Ulysses* as a whole, Bloom's wanderings providing a modern, sometimes mocking version of Odysseus's voyages in Homer's epic. In the latter part of the novel, Joyce also moves away from the mixture of subjective and objective registers discussed earlier to provide parodies of specific forms and styles – mocking or pastiching the language of science, of women's magazines, the catechism, journalism, popular fiction; and of various stages in the historical development of the English language itself. Joyce may have rewritten in *Ulysses* the definition of a man: he also rewrote writing and redefined definition, teasing and challenging the capacities of the word to represent the world. Constant parody and play install the means of representation – language and its particular colour and character – as a subject of the novel almost as central as the story it represents, or any character it is used to describe or define.

This interest is still more central to Joyce's later writing, which began to appear as 'Work in Progress' during the twenties. Set in the dreaming mind of a Dublin publican, 'Work in Progress' is in one way a final consummation of modernism's urge to look within the mind, moving beyond some of the limitations discussed above by creating a language extraordinary enough almost to represent a stream of unconsciousness. The language of 'Work in Progress', however, is so extraordinary that its representing, semantic function is almost overwhelmed by Joyce's extended, word-warping celebration of its other features and potentials – phonetic, etymological, musical, playful, inventive or metaphoric. Something of its nature is described and demonstrated in Joyce's phrase 'say mangraphique, may say nay por daguerre' (p.339). Typical in its punning parody of a famous saying, and in its inclusion of terms from Spanish and French as well as English, the phrase can also be deciphered to suggest that 'Work in Progress' is only 'graphique' – writing – rather than daguerrotype or any other primitive photographic attempt to represent the real world. This was more or less the conclusion one contemporary critic, Eugene Jolas, reached when along with Samuel Beckett and others he defended Joyce's work in a volume of essays, *Our Exagmination Round his Factification for Incamination of Work in Progress*, published in 1929. In an essay entitled 'The Revolution of Language and James Joyce', Jolas simply suggests that

> The epoch when the writer photographed the life about him with the mechanics of words redolent of the daguerrotype, is happily drawing to its close. The new artist of the word has recognised the autonomy of language.[15]

In fact, by 1929, it was modernism itself which was in some ways drawing to a close. Important novels remained to be published in the thirties – Virginia Woolf extends her interior monologue technique in *The Waves* (1931), and 'Work in Progress' was published complete as *Finnegans Wake* in 1939. And Finnegans, of course, never end but begin again: although *Finnegans Wake* in some ways marks a terminus or consummation of modernist energies and initiatives, it also helped develop them towards the later, postmodernist writing considered in Chapter Five. But modernist initiatives were in general replaced by other interests in the thirties, in ways discussed in the next chapter. Even in the twenties, modernism did not flourish to the exclusion of other more conventional forms of writing. The era of social change and shifting values which followed the First World War encouraged satire, for example, as well as the narrative experiment and innovation of the modernists. Aldous Huxley is in one way an experimental, modernist novelist – sustaining in *Point Counter Point* (1928) several different, counterpointed stories supposedly occurring simultaneously, but presented in successive blocks of narrative. He is also, however, more conventionally a satirist, teasing the bright young things of the Jazz Age in novels such as *Crome Yellow* (1921) and *Antic Hay* (1923), and providing in *Point Counter Point* some mildly satiric portraits of modernists such as D.H. Lawrence. The twenties were also a successful time for Ronald

Firbank. Novels such as *Valmouth* (1919), *Sorrow in Sunlight* (1924) and *Concerning the Eccentricities of Cardinal Pirelli* (1926) depict societies often imbued with Catholic faith but also exquisitely decadent, sharing some of the celebration of wit and hedonism in Norman Douglas's *South Wind* (1917) and looking back to Oscar Wilde and the 1890s. Yet in showing a certain darkness beneath social pretensions, and in relying extensively on dialogue and implication rather than authorial explanation, Firbank also looks forward, anticipating in style, wit and milieu the work of satirists and novelists of high society who followed in the thirties and later. One of these is Evelyn Waugh, who began with *Decline and Fall* (1928) his satiric treatment – rather like Huxley's – of bright young members of the lost generation after the war. This continues in thirties' novels further considered in Chapter Four, such as *Vile Bodies* (1930), *Black Mischief* (1932) and *Scoop* (1938).

Another novelist in some ways close to Firbank is Ivy Compton-Burnett. In *Pastors and Masters* (1925) she initiates interests which remained largely consistent through the eighteen novels which followed in a career lasting until the sixties. While Virginia Woolf saw human character changing in 1910, Compton-Burnett remarked that she had no real knowledge of life any later than 1910. The respectable, apparently trivial context of prosperous, late Victorian and Edwardian families is the constant setting of her novels; often – like much Edwardian fiction itself – concerned with the tyrannical domination of a parent. Such tyranny and cruel, claustrophobic family struggles for power place her fiction close – in subject and intensity of emotion, if not in mundane context – to the Greek tragedy she admired. A certain dramatic element also appears in her sometimes complete reliance on dialogue, requiring of readers as well as characters the acuteness to decipher implications and penetrate façades which conceal emotions running from petty jealousy in *Pastors and Masters* to murderous loathing in *A House and its Head* (1935). Concern with the penetration of façades and the minute analysis of motives place Compton-Burnett's fiction close to the work of Henry James as well as Firbank. The idiosyncrasy of her style and subject, however, make her an almost unique figure in English fiction.

Satire shows one area of fiction that continued relatively independent of modernism: some of the critics writing in the twenties also emphasise that modernism's hold on the contemporary imagination was much less than complete. Gerald Bullett, for example, in his study *Modern English Fiction* (1926), still considers Arnold Bennett, H.G. Wells, John Galsworthy and E.M. Forster among the most significant of living authors, while Joyce, Woolf, Lawrence and Dorothy Richardson receive attention only in a last chapter devoted to 'Eccentricities'. Most later critics would probably reverse Bullett's priorities, seeing Joyce, Woolf and Lawrence as the leading figures of their age, and modernist fiction itself as the most significant and influential new development in twentieth-century writing. Summing up the state of the novel in the fifties, Walter Allen found the modernists 'still the advance guard':[16] even as the century nears its end, this remains largely the case. New techniques modernist writers had established by the end of the twenties – whether for rendering subjective consciousness, restructuring the novel to resist the 'mechanical succession' of the clock, or otherwise amending the conventional form or language of fiction to meet particular needs – have proved useful for succeeding generations of novelists in various ways later chapters will examine.

Yet in another way Gerald Bullett's definition of the modernists as 'Eccentricities' remains appropriate. Rather than being entirely accepted into the mainstream of writing in Britain, the example of modernism has more often functioned as an alternative to it – even, as Allen suggests, a kind of permanent avant-garde – while the legacy of Victorian realism, carried forward by Wells, Bennett and Galsworthy, has remained an influence of at least equal strength. The extent to which modernism has seemed a worthwhile alternative influence has varied at different times later in the century, and neither novelists, critics nor readers have ever been unanimous in its praise. In particular, modernism was so successful in effacing the conditions of the modern industrial world which troubled its authors that it has always been open to the accusation that it ignores them altogether. The infinite inner reaches of mind and memory opened up by modernism did establish a vision of the self freed from forces threatening to reduce it to spiritless mechanism, but at the risk of omitting analysis of these forces themselves, or direct confrontation with them. History – the 'nightmare' Stephen Dedalus seeks to wake from in *Ulysses* – and its processes may seem simply avoided in favour of too close attention to inner, individual life rather than the problems of the social, public sphere. However conservative it has come to seem technically, the work of some of the novelists modernism rejected, such as H.G. Wells, does often confront the difficulties of contemporary society directly, even suggesting how these problems might be avoided. Moreover, modernist fiction's apparent evasion of this public world may at times seem to extend into a kind of evasion of the public itself, innovative styles and complexity of technique debarring it, more than most twentieth-century fiction, from the kind of wide readership writers such as H.G. Wells enjoyed.

Such potential limitations probably receive their most lucid, convincing summation in the criticism of Georg Lukács, who saw in modernism

> rejection of narrative objectivity, the surrender to subjectivity . . . disintegration of the outer world . . . the reduction of reality to a nightmare . . . the denial of history, of development, and thus of perspective.[17]

Lukács's criticisms appeared in his essay 'The Ideology of Modernism' in 1955: comparable views, however, were expressed much earlier, partly informing the reaction against modernism which began to appear distinctively in some of the fiction and criticism of the 1930s.

FURTHER READING

Malcolm Bradbury and James McFarlane (eds.) *Modernism 1890–1930*, Harmondsworth: Penguin, 1976.

Alan Friedman *The Turn of the Novel*, New York: Oxford University Press, 1966.

Robert Kiely *Beyond Egotism: The fiction of James Joyce, Virginia Woolf and D.H. Lawrence*, Cambridge, Massachusetts: Harvard University Press, 1980.

Michael Levenson *Modernism and the Fate of Individuality: Character and novelistic form from Conrad to Woolf*, Cambridge: Cambridge University Press, 1991.

George Parfitt *Fiction of the First World War: A study*, London: Faber, 1988.

Randall Stevenson *Modernist Fiction: An introduction*, Hemel Hempstead: Harvester Wheatsheaf, 1992.

3 *The Weather in the Streets*

The Thirties

Philip Henderson is one of the thirties critics who expresses views comparable to those of Georg Lukács quoted at the end of the last chapter. Writing in *The Novel Today: Studies in contemporary attitudes* (1936) from a Marxist point of view – like Lukács – Henderson complains that modernism was 'emmeshed in the chaos of subjectivism' and that it 'retired further and further into private worlds detached from social reality'. He also emphasises the novelist's responsibility for 'social being' rather than private experience by criticising Virginia Woolf's famous discussion, in her essay 'Mr. Bennett and Mrs. Brown' (1924), of how novelists might capture the character of a woman encountered in a railway compartment on a journey to London. Rather than trying as Woolf advocates to communicate this character's inner nature, Henderson suggests it would be more appropriate to 'glance out of the window at the street upon street of hovels converging upon London'.[1] His suggestion sums up a change in attitude and a reaction against modernism often in evidence in the thirties, a decade in which an inclination not to 'look within' but to 'glance out' on the city streets of contemporary society was widely shared. This change of direction and some of its likely causes are illustrated in the development of Christopher Isherwood's early career.

Isherwood's first two novels, *All the Conspirators* (1928) and *The Memorial* (1932), show extensive 'echoes', as he calls them, of the work of James Joyce and Virginia Woolf. In each novel, as in

Woolf's fiction, interior monologue often predominates over conversation and action. *All the Conspirators* also contains sections of randomly associating thoughts close to Joyce's stream of consciousness, and a concern with art and writing which resembles some of the self-consciousness of modernism. Affinities with modernism extend in *The Memorial* into areas of structure and temporality. The novel's four sections are headed 1928, 1920, 1925, and 1929: conventional chronology is further undermined by recollections and flashbacks which juxtapose the shallow, disillusioned gaiety following the First World War with what the novel calls 'the old safe, happy, beautiful world' (p.58) existing before it – a version of George Orwell's perpetual Edwardian summer in *Coming up for Air* (1939), quoted at the start of Chapter One. Isherwood later explained that in *The Memorial* 'time is circular, which sounds Einstein-ish and brilliantly modern'.[2]

Such 'brilliantly modern' techniques indicate the strength of modernist influence at the end of the twenties, but they disappear from Isherwood's writing fairly quickly and completely during the following decade. His next novel, *Mr Norris Changes Trains* (1935) has little of the structural complexity or inward registration of thought which distinguish his early fiction. Instead, *Mr Norris Changes Trains* is straightforward in chronology – following its narrator's gradual acquaintanceship with the sinister Mr Norris in Berlin – and objective in its detailed observation of characters' behaviour and the state of their city. *Goodbye to Berlin* (1939) is similar. Its preference for direct, uncomplicated contact with observed reality is emphasised by Isherwood's narrator, who claims 'I am a camera with its shutter open, quite passive, recording, not thinking' (p.11). 'Passive recording', of course, is never wholly realisable in the novel: just as a camera has to be pointed somewhere, any fiction is 'pointed' by language, style, point of view and much besides. Nevertheless, Isherwood's idea of the narrator as camera emphasises how far, by the end of the 1930s, his priorities had moved away from those of the modernists. Joseph Conrad, Henry James and Ford Madox Ford all welcomed the label 'impressionist' for their work; Virginia Woolf recommended following the 'myriad impressions' as they fell on the mind; Eugene Jolas suggested in 1929 that 'the epoch when the writer photographed . . . life' was over. Ten years later, Isherwood apparently wanted to reopen an epoch of photographic realism, reversing the priorities of the previous decade, directing the novel once again upon outward reality and social being rather than inner consciousness.

Several factors may have prompted Isherwood's change of style. Isherwood himself remarks that a fascination for the cinema made him 'endlessly interested in the outward appearance of people'.[3] Cinema's rapidly increasing popularity in the thirties made it a more general influence on novel-writing, its technique of cross-cutting perhaps encouraging the rapid alternation of short scenes which sometimes appears in the work of Evelyn Waugh and of Graham Greene, a regular film critic himself at this time. The principal incentive, however, for Isherwood's abandonment of the modernist manner of *The Memorial* might have been a wish to show the British public as clearly as possible the threat of Adolf Hitler – 'a *clever unscrupulous liar* [who] can deceive millions', as he is called in *Mr Norris Changes Trains* (p.188) – which Isherwood had discovered for himself on his visits to Berlin in the thirties. His lucid, documentary style provides a good vehicle for doing so. A narrator 'recording, not thinking' forces readers to judge for themselves dangers in the seductive, liberated but violent and corrupt city of Berlin. The fragmentary form of *Goodbye to Berlin* – a 'loosely connected sequence of diaries and sketches', as Isherwood calls it in his introduction – also emphasises the imminent collapse of a decadent city, ready and often willing to fall before the fascist threat.

Threats of this kind, of course, were hardly confined to Berlin at the time. In Italy, Mussolini's fascists had been in power since 1922. By 1936, they had overrun Abyssinia; Hitler had reoccupied the Rhineland, and General Franco's right-wing revolt against the legitimately elected Republican government had initiated civil war in Spain. Eventually involving many British volunteers, as well as German, Italian and Soviet forces, the Spanish Civil War deeply affected thirties opinion, especially among artists and writers, who saw in it an intensifying conflict between right and left, fascist and communist, which made wider European war inevitable. Graham Greene's *The Confidential Agent* (1939) suggests that the war in Spain would not be long in spreading to the rest of Europe. This expectation hardens into certainty for George Orwell in *Coming up for Air*, encouraging its nostalgia for idyllic earlier times. Throughout the decade, as Woolf suggests in her novel *Between the Acts* (1941), it was difficult to escape a 'vision of Europe, bristling with guns, poised with planes' and a sense of 'the doom of sudden death hanging over us . . . no retreating or advancing' (pp.43, 86).

Nor was this sense of doom, danger and difficulty confined to continental Europe. The collapse of the Wall Street stock market in 1929 brought the twenties to a very sharp close: it was quickly followed by the economic depression which facilitated Hitler's rise in Germany, but also greatly disturbed British affairs. By 1931, the pound had been devalued, the Labour Party ousted by a National Government created to deal with the emergency, and unemployment had risen to a level – surpassed in twentieth-century Britain only in the 1980s – which provoked hunger marches and the kind of riots, in Hyde Park, for example, which appear in Graham Greene's *It's a Battlefield* (1934).

History, in other words, was in many ways as much of a nightmare for members of the thirties generation as it had been for the modernists. But they had less inclination – and less opportunity – to awake from or otherwise evade it in ways the modernists had developed. Unlike the modernists, thirties writers lacked adult memories of a sunnier Edwardian past: significantly, it is to recollections only of Edwardian childhood and youth that Orwell returns in *Coming up for Air*. Equipped with clearer recollections of a better world in the past, the modernists restructured their fiction to retreat from a disturbed life after the First World War into inner consciousness – or through memory, the 'door' Lily Briscoe so often opens in Woolf's *To the Lighthouse* (1927), and which Joyce uses in his huge reconstruction in *Ulysses* (1922) of Dublin in 1904. Thirties authors, on the other hand, faced the difficulties of contemporary life and the threat of a future second war with less opportunity for 'retreating or advancing' in their novels. A greater obligation therefore fell upon them to consider how life could be restructured not only in fiction but in fact; to engage more directly with contemporary history; and to look at the political measures through which it might be changed. Virginia

Woolf summed up this new outlook in 1940, suggesting that
writers in the decade just ended had found it impossible not to
be interested in politics, not

> to be aware of what was happening in Russia; in Germany; in Italy;
> in Spain. They could not go on discussing aesthetic emotions and
> personal relations . . . they had to read the politicians. They read
> Marx. They became communists; they became anti-fascists.[4]

Later commentators have tended to confirm this picture of the
thirties as a time of strong political commitment among writers;
of an 'Auden generation' dominated by left-wing poets such as
Stephen Spender, Louis MacNeice, and W.H. Auden himself.
In fiction, similar commitments are seen underlying a movement away from personal or aesthetic interests and towards
broader social concern, often reflected in realist, even documentary styles. In the course of this chapter, it will become clear
that this general picture is in detail less than wholly accurate: in
style and in politics, thirties writers were less homogeneous
than it suggests. Nevertheless, in outline it is a view which does
define one of the more obvious trends of the decade, clarifying
the work not only of Isherwood but of several other contemporary authors.

One of these is George Orwell. Rather like Philip Henderson,
Orwell complained of modernism that it showed 'no attention to
the urgent problems of the moment, above all no politics in the
narrower sense'. Orwell's own commitment to the problems of
the moment appears in the 'meticulous descriptive quality',[5] as
he calls it, of early novels such as *A Clergyman's Daughter* (1935)
and *Keep the Aspidistra Flying* (1936), charting the kind of life on
or below the breadline whose discovery Orwell records in his
autobiographical *Down and Out in Paris and London* (1933). Such
social concerns also attracted him, like several of his contemporaries, to the authors modernism rejected. One popular thirties
writer, J.B. Priestley, looks back as far as Charles Dickens as an
inspiration for his grim account of London life in *Angel Pavement*
(1930). Walter Greenwood's popular *Love on the Dole* (1933) takes
one of its epigraphs from Arnold Bennett and shares his manner
of detailed presentation of an industrial landscape and its
deadening pressures: the warmth and resilience Greenwood
establishes for working-class characters is ultimately almost

overwhelmed by their monstrous environment. Orwell himself particularly admired H.G. Wells, adopting his strategy of following a character propelled by 'some unusual transverse force' through unfamilar social strata, exposing the particularities of each. Like the sudden wealth of Wells's hero in *Kipps* (1905), Dorothy's loss of memory in *A Clergyman's Daughter* allows Orwell to investigate a range of contemporary social problems as he charts her descent through various adventures to the life of the down-and-out. Sometimes thought a better journalist and essayist than a novelist, Orwell describes events in ways which often extend, as in Wells's writing, into sociological discussion of their general significance. Dorothy's gruelling time as a teacher, for example, introduces several paragraphs on 'the facts about private schools' (p.213), just as Wells temporarily deserts his story in *Tono-Bungay* (1909) to discuss the conditions of London housing.

Orwell's methods as essayist and novelist are probably best combined in *Coming up for Air*, in which the first-person narrator George Bowling helps combine social observation and personal experience more fully than in other novels. Bowling's slangy, colloquial familiarity, close to the tone of Orwell's non-fictional writing, also encourages readers' acquiescence in his opinions. His warm recollections of Edwardian life afford the novel the opportunity for what it calls 'looking at two worlds at once' (p.178), contrasting an idealised past with a commercialised, disorganised contemporary society, blind to the threat of Hitler and future war. This kind of threat the novel sees presaging a 'kind of hate-world, slogan-world. The coloured shirts, the barbed wire, the rubber truncheons' (p.149). Orwell considered most of his work written *'against* totalitarianism and *for* democratic socialism':[6] fears of the 'hate-world' of totalitarianism are most powerfully expressed in his best-known novel, *Nineteen Eighty-Four* (1949). Like Aldous Huxley's *Brave New World* (1932), *Nineteen Eighty-Four* is a prophetic, dystopian fantasy: Huxley, however, demonstrates the dangers of amoral scientific progress, whereas Orwell projects his political fears into an imaginary future Britain under the tyrannical rule of Big Brother. The political fable *Animal Farm* (1945) further expresses a particular horror of Stalin's totalitarianism – one which Orwell acquired in encounters with Soviet forces while fighting in the

Spanish Civil War, an experience he documents in *Homage to Catalonia* (1938). The nature of Stalin's regime and its purges had already been revealed to British readers by Arthur Koestler's partly-documentary account of imprisonment and brainwashing in *Darkness at Noon* (1940).

Orwell once described Graham Greene as belonging to the 'mild left', with 'faint leanings' towards communism.[7] Greene's left-wing allegiance may have seemed mild to Orwell, but it was firm enough to shape much of his thirties fiction and to remain in evidence in one way or another throughout his very long career. It appears in later life in Greene's friendships with Ho Chi Minh, Fidel Castro and General Torrijos of Panama, and in several novels set in areas of political struggle – Vietnam for *The Quiet American* (1955), for example; Cuba for *Our Man in Havana* (1958); Haiti for *The Comedians* (1966). Critics, however, have more often concentrated on the significance for Greene's fiction of the Catholic faith to which he was converted in 1926. This does become a central interest in novels often held to be Greene's best achievement – *Brighton Rock* (1938), *The Power and the Glory* (1940), *The Heart of the Matter* (1948), and *The End of the Affair* (1951) – yet even in these novels religious issues do not exclude political or humane ones, but often coexist and compete with them. In *The Power and the Glory*, for example, a dual allegiance underlies the conflict of the Priest and the Lieutenant, fired by his idealistic vision of a better society created by political reform. The same conflict is still more explicit forty years later in the debates between a priest and a communist ex-mayor which take up much of *Monsignor Quixote* (1982).

As Greene himself remarks, Catholicism is in any case invisible in his novels before *Brighton Rock*, and his fiction in the thirties – like his cousin Christopher Isherwood's work – undergoes changes of style and priority partly in response to the contemporary political world. Unlike Isherwood, however, Greene renounced the idiom not of modernism but of romance. Though showing a characteristic interest in betrayal and pursuit, his first novels – *The Man Within* (1929), *The Name of Action* (1930), *Rumour at Nightfall* (1931) – are romantic, historical dramas about smuggling, gun-running and the like. Greene later rejected them: by *Stamboul Train* (1932) he had adopted the kind of contemporary setting, in a graceless, usually urban world, which reappears throughout the rest of his fiction. Disconsolate and seedy in ways often metaphoric of the spiritlessness of their inhabitants, such settings are both recognisably realistic and yet sufficiently distinctive to have generated the critical term 'Greeneland' to describe them. Throughout his writing, they are vividly communicated by a prose shaped by the preference for 'straight sentences, no involutions . . . present[ing] the outside world economically and exactly' which Greene records having learned at an early stage of his career, perhaps from his work as a newspaper sub-editor. Greene also remarks of his move from romance to realism that 'reality, blessed reality, broke through in the form of financial anxiety'.[8] Personal anxieties of this kind during the thirties may also have helped dispose Greene towards the political vision of *It's a Battlefield*, which examines an inequitable society run by 'kings and priests and lawyers and rich men' (p.97), and the approval for Republican Spain which appears in *The Confidential Agent*.

The unusual, sophisticated quality of *The Confidential Agent* also reflects Greene's 'ambition to create something legendary out of a contemporary thriller'.[9] His hero, D., is a shy, mildly incompetent lecturer in Medieval French, an expert on *The Song of Roland*: an unlikely figure to be thrown into international espionage and intrigue. Exploration of the stresses which result leads Greene to explore character, morals and relationships with a depth and seriousness unusual in the thriller form. It is nevertheless typical of Greene's development of this form in thirties novels such as *Stamboul Train* and *A Gun for Sale* (1936), as well as later works such as *The Human Factor* (1978): one of Greene's most influential achievements is the creation of a new substance and seriousness for the thriller. Another, however, is his strengthening of elements of pace and thrill within what is usually considered more substantial and serious fiction. Even when writing outwith the spy or thriller genres, Greene usually employs a strong, exciting story as a vehicle for investigating morals and character, extending into later twentieth-century writing the manner of authors he admired, such as Joseph Conrad and Robert Louis Stevenson.

The Confidential Agent illustrates another reason for Greene's wide appeal: the survival from his early novels of an element of romance, even within the spiritless settings of his later writing. In some novels, this element directs a subsidiary narrative, counterpointed with his fiction's more central vision of a thoroughly mundane reality. This tactic is employed most obviously in *The End of the Affair*, which includes two highly contrasting versions of the same events – Sarah's committed to the divine and miraculous, while her lover Bendrix, the novel's main narrator, emphasises the sexual and secular. In *The Confidential Agent*, frequent reference to the romantic heroism of *The Song of Roland* highlights by contrast the seediness of life in the thirties, but also emphasises by analogy D.'s retention of heroic courage and integrity despite his own shortcomings and the grey disillusion of his world. This kind of division or doubling in narrative extends a divided, paradoxical quality Greene himself identifies in his moral vision as a whole. He suggests that the interest of his fiction in general is in 'The dangerous edge of things/The honest thief, the tender murderer/The superstitious atheist'.[10] Showing honesty, tenderness and virtue paradoxically surviving under the constant shadow of dishonesty, violence and betrayal, Greene's concentration on such morally ambiguous figures has a particular appropriateness – and a particular appeal – for the age his fiction surveyed, in the thirties and since. Thinking in *The End of the Affair* about the kind of heroic figures idealised in the Edwardian period, such as Captain Scott, Bendrix remarks that 'it seemed curiously dated now, this heroism . . . Two wars stood between us and them' (p.173). In the disillusioned century Bendrix describes, Greene's half-romantic realism is ideally equipped to create a compromised but credible heroism. This vision helped to make him one of the most popular – as well as critically admired – novelists of his age.

However firm his political commitments in the thirties and since, Greene was a member of the Communist Party for only four weeks, while a student at Oxford in 1925. Other authors to be considered later – Edward Upward, Rex Warner, L.H. Myers, Lewis Grassic Gibbon – provide firmer evidence than Isherwood, Greene or Orwell for Woolf's claim that thirties writers read Marx and became communists. There were, in any case, some contemporary novelists whose allegiances clearly lay in the opposite direction. Wyndham Lewis registered approval for Mussolini in one of his analyses of twenties culture, *The Art of Being Ruled* (1926), and he went on to publish a sympathetic account of Hitler in 1931. Though he later realised his error where Hitler was concerned, right-wing sympathies continued to inform his thirties writing. *The Revenge for Love* (1937) attacks again the kind of phoney art world satirised in *The Apes of God* (1930), but also what Lewis saw as pretentious political affectations and a fake, fashionable response to the war in Spain. 'False Bottoms' was his original title for the novel, and everything in it has one. A Spaniard even describes his nation and Britain as 'two countries going rotten at the bottom' (p.6). Only Margaret's love for the phoney artist Victor is exempt from pervasive pretentiousness. This relationship is presented with an inwardness unusual in Lewis's fiction: combined with his more habitual 'external method', discussed in Chapter Two, this makes *The Revenge for Love* one of his best novels.

Like Wyndham Lewis, Evelyn Waugh was firmly disposed against the general trend of contemporary commitments: he indicated support for General Franco in 1937, and the travelogue *Waugh in Abyssinia* (1936) shows some sympathy for Mussolini's fascists and their African ambitions. Such attitudes occasionally extend into his thirties fiction: like *The Revenge for Love*, the newspaper satire *Scoop* (1938) mocks English communists as 'University Men', parodies speeches on behalf of the proletariat and attacks the kind of support the British public extended to Republican Spain. Waugh was as fascinated as Lewis by what he saw as bogusness and pretension, but remained more concerned with its social rather than overtly political forms. His thirties fiction (further considered in Chapter Four) concentrates on the kind of insouciant, hedonistic society first satirised in *Decline and Fall* (1928) – one into which serious issues, political or other, are rarely allowed to intrude.

So all thirties writers did not move in the direction of left-wing politics: even those who did were not uniformly attracted to the kind of 'camera-eye' directness exemplified by Isherwood. In his 'London Trilogy' *Twenty Thousand Streets Under the Sky* (1935), Patrick Hamilton does offer an example of grimly realistic portrayal of contemporary working-class life, sharpened by its author's Marxism and 'the exact and intimate knowledge' of the 'brick and concrete jungle' for which J.B. Priestley praised him.[11] Lewis Jones likewise used a first-hand knowledge of communist politics in the Welsh coalfields in *We Live* (1939): the realism of his account of the General Strike and the struggles which followed also figures in the work of fellow Welsh novelists concerned with mining life, in the thirties and later, such as Rhys Davies. Other contemporary authors, however, found the conflicts and commitments generated by the crises of the thirties best communicated not by a style which 'present[s] the outside world economically and exactly' but by following the same path as Orwell's later fiction towards fantasy and allegory. Rex Warner, for example, remarks 'I do not even aim at realism'.[12] Though his first novel, *The Wild Goose Chase* (1937), is clearly concerned with the fascist movements of the thirties, the General Strike, and the British Government's attempt to appease Hitler rather than re-arming, these and other contemporary events are all projected onto a level of allegory and fantasy. The novel ends in a kind of Marxist wish-fulfilment, with a communist state created out of the ruins of the warped, amorphous world in which the novel opens. Warner's movements between reality and fantasy, however, are at times confused and awkward, and *The Wild Goose Chase* sometimes seems amorphous and long enough itself to make its title only too appropriate. Warner's fantasy and satire are more pointedly concentrated in a novel popular in the early years of the war, *The Aerodrome* (1941), which finds an exact device for examining contemporary conflicts between democracy and fascism. These are contextualised in Warner's contrast of a lively, disorderly village with the soulless efficiency of the air force stationed nearby; of 'ordinary life' with 'perfect efficiency . . . iron compulsion' (pp.136, 261).

Warner acknowledged the influence of Franz Kafka, four of whose novels first appeared in English translation during the thirties. Something of Kafka's vision of dark, threatening worlds, warped by the uneasy imaginations of his protagonists, also appears in the writing of Edward Upward. As an escape from their actual experience of Cambridge University in the twenties, Upward developed with his friend Christopher Isherwood a private fantasy domain, Mortmere: this later figures in his volume of short stories, *The Railway Accident* (1961).

An element of Mortmere-like fantasy also appears in *Journey to the Border* (1938), Upward's hero finding himself in 'a sort of no-man's-land' (p.202) between sanity and insanity, illusion and actuality, in which other characters appear as alarming freaks. He retains just enough sanity to arrest his mental deterioration – strongly communicated by Upward's confinement of the narrative to his interior monologue – by concluding that the only way to regain reality is to 'get in touch with the workers' movement . . . there is no other way of dealing *successfully* with the real external problems' (pp.213, 215). Much the same conclusion is reached by the hero of Upward's later *In the Thirties* (1962), who joins the Communist Party as a refuge from a failed career as a poet and to make common cause with others frustrated by the social and economic conditions of the time. *In the Thirties* gives a broadly realistic picture of these conditions – unemployment, poverty, political activism, pacifism, mass demonstrations – while *Journey to the Border* indicates how deeply such issues remained implicated even in fiction whose fantastic style might have been expected to move it away from concern with contemporary reality.

This is also evident even in the work of L.H. Myers, whose tetralogy *The Near and the Far* (1929–40) apparently renounces the contemporary in favour of a setting in sixteenth-century India. Myers, however, explains in his preface that it was never his intention 'to set aside the social and ethical problems that force themselves upon us at the present time'. His remote, romantic setting is used to add objectivity to an assessment of what are often very much the issues which particularly preoccupied the thirties, as well as the investigation of the nature of government in general. In the last volume, *The Pool of Vishnu*, for example, Myers presents a vision of the communist ideals of the thirties more plausible than Warner's *The Wild Goose Chase*, showing the redistribution of resources within a state then run as a co-operative commune. Its ideals and theories, however, are the work of a Guru who emphasises Myers's interest in religion and spirituality as well as contemporary politics and the immediate problems of the everyday world. Religion concerns many of his characters, and the competing claims of Buddhism, Hinduism and Christianity are often debated at length. A symbolic aspect to many episodes and scenes helps integrate this dimension of ideas and abstract thought within a complex, colourful plot, full of intrigue, surprise and puzzle. *The Near and the Far* is often an entertaining novel as well as a serious, philosophic one: much admired in the thirties, it deserves wider attention from later readers.

George Orwell saw as typical of the thirties a 'need for *something to believe in*' as an antidote to the stresses of contemporary life.[13] Rather like Graham Greene, L.H. Myers shows how this need extended towards religion as well as – sometimes alongside – politics. Some of John Cowper Powys's work is similarly oriented. Powys published around twenty novels during a long career, some of the best of them – such as *Wolf Solent* (1929), *A Glastonbury Romance* (1932), *Weymouth Sands* (1934) and *Maiden Castle* (1936) – appearing around the thirties. Each is set in Wessex, where Powys grew up. He dedicated his first novel, *Wood and Stone* (1915), to another Wessex novelist, Thomas Hardy, equally committed to the primordial life and values of the country. Like his brother T.F. Powys, however – whose *Mr Weston's Good Wine* (1927) shows God visiting an ordinary English village in the guise of a wine salesman – John Cowper Powys is concerned not only with the natural world and intense personal relationships within it, but with the supernatural; with religion, pagan or Christian, and its connection to the everyday. The opening sentences of *A Glastonbury Romance*, for example, emphasise that the novel is set both 'within a causal radius of Brandon railway-station and yet beyond the deepest pools of emptiness between the uttermost stellar systems' and that the novel is concerned not only with 'the soul of a particular human-being' but with 'the divine-diabolic soul of the First Cause of all life'. The pages which follow do remain close to some of the conflicts of the thirties, which appear, for example, in a struggle between capitalists and communists. But the novel is also very extensively concerned with 'divine-diabolic' forces encountered by its hero on a walk from Glastonbury to Stonehenge. Powys's determination to examine spiritual, magical and secular forms of such forces occupies twelve hundred pages of complicated plot and a cast of around fifty very strangely named characters. The huge range of this interest in forms and forces ruling life – from beyond as well as within its everyday surface – ensures a continuing appeal for

Powys's fiction, especially among later generations of readers attracted to mysticism and the occult, though critics remain divided about Powys's literary merit.

Though in different ways, Lewis Grassic Gibbon's trilogy *A Scots Quair* is also structured around commitment to immediate history and to factors which lie beyond it. Gibbon reflects the effects of the First World War within a rural community in *Sunset Song* (1932); the failure of the General Strike in *Cloud Howe* (1933); and the consequent hardening of attitudes into the thirties communism for which his hero Ewan agitates in the urban context of *Grey Granite* (1934). Ewan's mother, however, also includes in her feelings for the land she works in her youth a sense of its eternal quality, its endurance beyond the immediate struggles of human life. This eternal quality in the land is emphasised by the ancient Standing Stones which preside over it and represent in the novel the ideal of a lost Golden Age. Ewan's commitment to the immediate – to 'LIVING HISTORY ONESELF, being it, making it' – partly contrasts with this ideal, but also partly supports it through faith that the kind of ideal age 'without gods and classes' which was lost in the past can also, through political action, be re-created in the future (*Grey Granite*, pp.161, 48). The novel's adroit structure – chapters are circular, beginning just after the sequence of events they go on to describe – supports this sense of an immediate historical experience which may be contained and directed by a larger vision. At many stages this double focus also intensifies the novel's emotions: for example, at the end of *Sunset Song*, when the loss of the Edwardian age and the more distant Golden Age is interconnected by the carving into the Standing Stones of a memorial for those killed in the First World War – 'the Last of the Peasants, the last of the Old Scots folk' (*Sunset Song*, p.252).

The life of these peasants, and of city-dwellers, is communicated with unusual breadth and intimacy in *A Scots Quair*. In this area, like D.H. Lawrence – whose work *A Scots Quair* sometimes resembles – Gibbon probably benefited from belonging to the class and community he came to write about. Much of the thirties fiction discussed so far can be seen as conditioned and in some ways limited by the public-school, Oxford or Cambridge backgrounds shared by most of its authors.[14] Such backgrounds kept these writers at a distance from the kind of working life towards which their politics inclined them, perhaps making inevitable their roles as mere camera-like observers; distanced documentarists of an existence from which class and education left them partly aloof. Gibbon, on the other hand, shows working life from the inside, using a range of interior monologues to communicate the thoughts and feelings not only of a few principal characters, but to give access to many members of rural and urban communities. The kind of Free Indirect Style characteristic of D.H. Lawrence's fiction – very flexibly employed – allows Gibbon to alternate the novel's attention very freely between many individuals, and at times to develop a kind of choric voice for the community as a whole. This communality of insight and speech, along with a structure which follows both immediate political conflicts and the kind of vision which could create an ideal future beyond them, make *A Scots Quair* probably the most powerful of all thirties novels – one of very few to develop the form of fiction in order to find strategies specifically appropriate to the experience and idealism of its age.

The outstanding achievement of *A Scots Quair* is part of a wider renaissance in Scottish writing which appeared in the late twenties and thirties. In the novel, this included Eric Linklater's early fiction, such as the satiric *Juan in America* (1931) and *Magnus Merriman* (1934); Compton Mackenzie's huge romantic and personal history, *The Four Winds of Love* (8 vols., 1937–45), which reflects many of the political and religious conflicts of the thirties and earlier; Naomi Mitchison's *The Corn King and the Spring Queen* (1931); and the work of Neil Gunn. Rather like *A Scots Quair*, Gunn's *Highland River* (1937), for example, follows growth from childhood to maturity in a rural community. It also shares some of Lewis Grassic Gibbon's faith in an ancient Scottish landscape as a setting in which the immediate shock of the First World War and the advancing pressures of the modern age may be escaped or transcended. Like Joseph Conrad's Marlow in *Heart of Darkness* (1902), Gunn's hero eventually embarks on a journey upriver which is in part a journey into the self: it is also, however, a journey beyond it, into an unfettered dimension, outwith time, history and society, which the land has come to represent in the novel. Like the writing of several novelists of the Renaissance – James Barke offers another example in *The Land of the Leal* (1939) – through renewed visions of history and Scottish rural life Gunn's fiction moves at times towards myth.

Sharing in some of the contemporary development of Scottish writing, Gibbon's work also illustrates – especially in its amendment of conventional fictional chronology, and its extension of registers for inner thought – the legacy of modernist interests which survived into the thirties despite movements in contrary directions at the time. Much thirties writing did move away from innovation and formal experiment, but as suggested earlier – and illustrated by the examples of Myers, Powys and several others – the movement was not always towards conventional realism; nor, as *A Scots Quair* indicates, always very far away from modernism at all. A limited modernist inheritance remains apparent – if only occasionally – even among authors whose social or political interests most favoured economic and exact presentation of 'the outside world'. Graham Greene, for example, flirts with stream of consciousness and interior monologue in the early part of *England Made Me* (1935), while George Orwell presents his heroine's nocturnal adventures in *A Clergyman's Daughter* in a semi-surreal dialogue form based on James Joyce's tactics in the 'Nighttown' chapter (15) of *Ulysses*.

A modernist manner turns up in some other unexpected quarters at the time. Throughout his long career, stretching back to *Liza of Lambeth* in 1897, Somerset Maugham is generally considered conservative in outlook and technique, though there is some departure from this manner in his study of good, evil and religion in *The Razor's Edge* (1944). *Cakes and Ale* (1930) – Maugham's own favourite among his works – extends the kind of self-consciousness about technique and construction which appears in *The Razor's Edge*, adding a further modernist interest in the past and how it can be recovered through memory. Discussion and demonstration of the falsifications of fiction, memory and biography create a novel complex in structure and chronology, resembling Ford Madox Ford's *The Good Soldier* (1915) and engagingly illustrating the range of formal possibilities modernism had made available by the end of the twenties.

The work of other contemporary writers is more consistently shaped by adoption of modernist methods and interests. Jean

Rhys was directly in contact with several modernist authors in Paris in the twenties and follows in her fiction randomly associating, unfolding thoughts much in the manner of Joyce. Rhys, however, not only inherits but develops modernist technique. *Good Morning, Midnight* (1939), for example, communicates the musing inner life of a lonely, uncertain heroine, adrift in the Paris of the Lost Generation, in a mixture of immediate consciousness and memory, sometimes transcribed in the past tense, sometimes in the present – a fluent, haunting form which is distinctively Rhys's own.

Two other writers in the thirties, Elizabeth Bowen and Rosamond Lehmann, show in their fiction the effects of admiration for Virginia Woolf. Bowen saw communication of what she calls an 'intense inner existence' as a particular strength of Woolf's fiction,[15] and employs interior monologue extensively in her own work to illumine what *The House in Paris* (1935) refers to as 'the you inside you . . . reflections . . . memories' (p.77). Bowen's tripartite division of *The House in Paris* – into two parts dealing with a single day in the present, with a section of past experience inserted between them – also rather resembles the structure of Woolf's *To the Lighthouse* (1927). Bowen uses this structure to highlight the effect of guilty, tangled past relations on a younger generation of children. This interest in the encounter of innocent childhood with guilty adult experience is continued in *The Death of the Heart* (1938), also extending Bowen's admiration for Henry James, perhaps particularly his use of a child's point of view in *What Maisie Knew* (1897).

Rosamond Lehmann's debts to modernism are probably clearest in her third novel, *The Weather in the Streets* (1936), a sequel to *Invitation to the Waltz* (1932). Rather like Dorothy Richardson, Lehmann uses both first- and third-person forms of narrative: whereas Richardson moves between them within single paragraphs, however, Lehmann's alternations occur between the various sections of the novel. Parts One, Three and Four are narrated from a third-person authorial perspective, while her heroine Olivia's first-person narrative is followed in Part Two. This change of tactics heightens the immediacy with which Olivia's clandestine relationship is presented at the stage when it has reached its maximum intimacy and happiness.

Emotional experience, however, is strongly communicated throughout, Lehmann's creation for her heroine of a half-conversational, reflective inner voice establishing 'an intensely concentrated inner life of thought and feeling' (p.211), as the novel calls it, which resembles Woolf's work as much as Richardson's. The depth and frankness with which – from a woman's point of view – Lehmann highlights emotions surrounding a complex, painful affair make *The Weather in the Streets* an outstanding, unusual thirties novel. As Woolf suggests, under the pressure of public affairs, personal emotions and relationships fade from the centre of novelists' attention during the decade. Only William Gerhardie's *Of Mortal Love* (1936) matches the depth of Lehmann's concentration on the power, strangeness and irresolution of emotional affairs and love. Gerhardie, however, strangely mixes seriousness and levity. His wry, idiosyncratic tone has continued to appeal to later novelists such as Olivia Manning, C.P. Snow and William Cooper.

Rhys, Bowen and Lehmann offer in the thirties an early illustration of an aspect of women's writing which remains in evidence throughout the century: its particular readiness to adopt and extend the innovative fictional strategies of modernism – often, of course, the invention of women in the first place. Several male authors in the thirties, however, also showed early forms of the extension of modernist methods. Malcolm Lowry's *Ultramarine* (1933) – a kind of Portrait of the Artist as a Young Seaman – is almost overwhelmed by a diversity of modernist styles: stream of consciousness, interior monologue, intrusive memories, changes of perspective and Joycean wordplay. Samuel Beckett, in *Murphy* (1938), and Flann O'Brien in *At Swim-Two-Birds* (1939) extend in more measured ways the example of Joyce, while in *The Black Book* (1938) Lawrence Durrell develops some of the methods and interests of D.H. Lawrence and of the Paris-based American writer Henry Miller.

The main achievement and influence of these writers came later in the century, and is considered in Chapter Five. The appearance of their early work during the decade, however, alongside some of the other novels discussed above, further suggests that the conventional critical picture of the thirties – of an 'Auden generation' – needs to be amended to take account of some of these extraAudenary elements. Although many novelists shared Isherwood's movement away from innovative styles and forms, modernism was by no means eclipsed in the thirties. On the contrary, the decade contained within a single period not only the kind of preferences – for social issues and conventional styles – which had generally distinguished the Edwardian age, but also at least a continuing element of the experimentation with form and style which had appeared in its modernist successor. The thirties, in other words, contained an early form of the crossroads of conflicting possibilities, of choices between tradition and innovation, which Chapter Five suggests directed the development of British fiction later in the century. Before any of that development could take place, however, the Second World War intervened, redirecting and reshaping the novel's subjects and structures and, like the First, continuing to influence life and literature for many years after actual hostilities had ceased.

FURTHER READING

Bernard Bergonzi *Reading the Thirties*, London: Macmillan, 1978.
Valentine Cunningham *British Writers of the Thirties*, Oxford: Oxford University Press, 1988.
James Gindin *British Fiction in the 1930s*, London: Macmillan, 1992.
Samuel Hynes *The Auden Generation: Literature and politics in England in the 1930s*, London: The Bodley Head, 1976.
Richard Johnstone *The Will to Believe: Novelists of the nineteen-thirties*, Oxford: Oxford University Press, 1982.

4 *Shadows in Eden*

The War Years to the Fifties

Not surprisingly, the period of the war seemed at the time – and has often been considered since – an almost insurmountably difficult one for writing. George Orwell talked in 1940 of 'the *impossibility* of any major literature until the world has shaken itself into its new shape'. The novelist P.H. Newby wondered in 1951

> whether so overwhelming and universal a catastrophe as the late war can be reckoned the sort of experience out of which an artist can create. What . . . can he do with it?

In his study of wartime writing, one later commentator, Robert Hewison, simply states that 'the war was a depressing time . . . the next years were to be worse'.[1] This chapter will suggest, on the contrary, that the threatening, overwhelming, depressing nature of the war and the years that followed certainly did not obliterate fiction, as Newby almost suggests. Instead, it provoked and challenged the contemporary imagination into particular – and productive – reshapings of narrative considered below, contributing to a fairly successful period for the novel; certainly a distinctive one.

The difficulties for authors at the time were nevertheless genuine, and unavoidable. Some were simply practical. Writers' homes or places of work were destroyed (much of Graham Greene's house in Clapham, for example, was demolished by a bomb); paper was in short supply and its use for literary publishing severely restricted; large stocks of books were wiped out during the Blitz of 1940–1; and the war's 'overwhelming' events were sometimes expected to distract readers' attention from fiction altogether. In fact, as Evelyn Waugh records in his trilogy reflecting wartime experience, *Sword of Honour* (1952–61), the war was 'a golden age for the book-trade, anything sold' (p.416) – unusually long periods of enforced idleness, in the armed forces and elsewhere, creating a brisk new market for novels.

The most significant difficulties in writing them, however, were in any case not so much practical as imaginative. The bombing raids of the Blitz, for example, were an experience whose strangeness threatened to outstrip anything fiction could offer, or the imagination contain. One contemporary commentator, Tom Harrisson, suggested that 'books pale into stupidity beside the real thing': several others record a strange sense that 'the real thing' – actual wartime experience – seemed fantastic, imaginary or dream-like, as if somehow already a kind of fiction itself. In her novel of life during the Blitz, *The Heat of the Day* (1949), Elizabeth Bowen describes 'that heady autumn of the first London air raids' as 'phantasmagoric . . . apocryphal' (pp.90–2). Reflecting some of his own wartime work in the Auxiliary Fire Service – in a short story published in the wartime journal *Penguin New Writing* – Henry Green likewise talks of contemporary life existing on 'a frontier of hopes or mostly fears' somewhere beyond 'a web of dreams'. If it did not make novels seem actually redundant, pale or stupid, this fabulous, fictional aspect to contemporary reality at least complicated their structuring of experience. As Tom Harrisson goes on to comment, once 'life's events' had been taken over by 'pressures of gigantic war', they sometimes seemed too strange or dream-like for the novelist 'to work . . . into the familiar patterns'.[2]

This difficulty with conventional patterning – or even with recording experience of the war in ordinary language at all – is illustrated by one of the best of wartime novels, Henry Green's *Caught* (1943). Much of the novel is taken up with its hero Richard Roe's wearisome inactivity as an auxiliary fireman during the quiet early days of the war, the 'Great Bore War' as Evelyn Waugh calls it in his dedication to *Put out More Flags* (1942). When the first air raids bring this phase of the war to an

end, Roe comments that what goes on in London seems 'like a
film . . . everything seems unreal', adding that 'the point about
a blitz is this, there's always something you can't describe'
(pp.174, 179–80). Green emphasises such difficulties of description by juxtaposing Roe's spoken account of events with the
unspoken thoughts which appear throughout the novel
enclosed in parentheses:

> 'The first night,' he said, 'we were ordered to the docks. As we came
> over Westminster Bridge it was fantastic, the whole of the left side of
> London seemed to be alight'.
>   (It had not been like that at all . . . the sky in that quarter, which
> happened to be the east . . . was flooded in a second sunset, orange
> and rose, turning the pavements pink . . .) (p.176)

As well as demonstrating in this way some of the difficulties
of narrating the overwhelming experience of the war, *Caught*
indicates a possible solution – the presentation, as in the extract
above, of violent action through the mind and language of a
character whose uncertain response to events helps communicate something of their strangeness. Along with some of the
other novels considered below, *Caught* helps in this way to
answer P.H. Newby's question about what – if anything – the
artist could do with the experience of the war. *Caught*, however,
also illustrates strengths and characteristics of Green's writing
which extend well beyond wartime, appearing in one form or
another throughout his career. The idle scenes in Roe's fire
station exemplify his talent for establishing arrays of emotions,
tensions, suspicions and affections within a group of people
'caught' together in situations of work or leisure. Green's early
novel *Living* (1929), centred on a small group of workers in a
Midlands factory, is another example of this interest in everyday
routine and ritual. *Living* also illustrates the unusualness of
Green's fictional language, often employing a form of Free
Indirect Style which keeps the narrative close, in this case, to the
spoken idiom of its Midlands characters. Actual dialogue and
direct speech is also used extensively – almost exclusively in
Green's last two novels, *Nothing* (1950) and *Doting* (1952). Like
Ivy Compton-Burnett's work, such writing challenges readers to
decipher significances and implications in a narrative from
which authorial comment is often largely absent. This challenge

is extended – most noticeably in *Loving* (1945) and *Concluding* (1948) – by Green's habit of constructing symbolic episodes, or juxtaposing scenes, in ways suggestive of a meaning or pattern which nevertheless remains unstated and sometimes indecipherable. Green himself considered that the novelist should 'communicate obliquely with his readers', since 'life is oblique in its impact upon people'.[3] The oblique, sometimes puzzling quality of his fiction probably accounts for his lack of a wide readership, despite general critical acclaim. It is nevertheless balanced by a warm, consistent humour and a wry affirmation of life and loving as well as the tangled perplexities of the world. In particular, Green provides one of the least pessimistic of contemporary visions of the effects of war in *Back* (1946). This moves towards the atmosphere of romance, showing a hero finding in a new relationship some compensation for the pain and chaos of the war, and an almost magical restoration of the lover he lost during it.

Rather than being only depressing or overwhelming, the war and the following years were unusually productive for Green, who published more fiction in the forties than at any other time in his career – perhaps because the habitual strategies of his writing particularly equipped him to respond to the war's challenge to conventional patterns and structures in the novel. Other writers successful in communicating the strangeness of wartime experience often share something of Green's tactics of defamiliarisation and obliqueness. In *No Directions* (1943), for example, the prolific novelist James Hanley presents the events of a single Blitz night in a London tenement largely through the disturbed minds of the various occupants. The title is appropriate. As in Green's novels, there are few authorial directions to the reader, and swift alternation among a variety of confused, fearful, hasty responses to events challenges readers' comprehension in a manner at least loosely analogous to the shock to perception and understanding experienced by characters caught up in the actual events of the war.

P.H. Newby's fiction is similarly disorienting, sometimes suggesting, like Henry Green's, the incapacity of ordinary language to represent the war's bewildering violence. In Newby's *The Retreat* (1953), for example – sequel to *A Step to Silence* (1952) – the bombing of his hero Oliver's ship in the withdrawal from Dunkirk cannot be easily followed in the chaotic, incompletely realised account the novel provides of it. This dramatises Oliver's sense that 'he had lost contact' (p.34) with normal reality and helps create an impression typical in Newby's fiction – of the recording of events as they impinge on characters' minds, at the very moment of perception, before they have time for reflection or assessment. Readers are obliged to engage along with characters in the difficult process of making sense of what is happening to them, sharing Oliver's feeling in *The Retreat* that 'a strange pattern was being presented, but no matter how quickly his eye moved the pattern never fell within his field of vision' (p.60). This sense of displaced meaning and fractured pattern makes Newby's fiction ideally adapted – like Henry Green's – to communicate the dream-like strangeness of the war, although it is actually a fairly constant feature of his writing throughout his career. It is later used to emphasise the chaos of another conflict – the Suez crisis of 1956 – in *Something to Answer For* (1968). As in *The Retreat*, readers share with a central character the task of differentiating reality and hallucination in a setting whose political crisis and dream-like disintegration make the two states peculiarly difficult to distinguish.

Writing in 1946, Rosamond Lehmann concluded that *Caught* was 'one important exception' to her view that no great war novel had yet appeared; Green alone having 'succeeded in coming to terms with the times' by 'translating fresh experience, the direct result of war, into an adequate pattern'.[4] Neither *Caught*, however, nor the fiction of Newby – nor of many other successful writers at the time – can be altogether accurately described as translating experience which is the *direct* result of the war, in the sense of actual military action. The Blitz figures only briefly in the last section of *Caught*, while in *The Retreat* Oliver quickly escapes from the chaos of Dunkirk to the depths of the English countryside. Military life and action do figure convincingly in a number of novels at the time – in *From the City, From the Plough* (1948), Alexander Baron's account of an infantry battalion's training and its combat after the Normandy landings; occasionally in Eric Linklater's *Private Angelo* (1946); and in some of Evelyn Waugh's vision of the gradual doom of idealism in a violent, unprincipled world in *Sword of Honour*. But as Anthony

Burgess has suggested, even long after Rosamond Lehmann's judgement in 1946 little British fiction has appeared which reflects the nightmare destruction and violence of the war so extensively and vividly as American novels, such as Norman Mailer's *The Naked and the Dead* (1948), Joseph Heller's *Catch-22* (1960) or Thomas Pynchon's *Gravity's Rainbow* (1973).

Only a narrow definition of war fiction, however, would consider it confined to novels which reflect violence, combat and military action directly or exclusively. As the critic Walter Allen points out,

> No rigid distinction between war novels and others is possible . . . Since war was the inescapable experience of everyone, civilians as much as soldiers, we find the war present throughout the fiction of the forties and the decades that follow, not necessarily shown directly but there as the ineluctable shadow under which characters and events have their being.[5]

In the ways Allen indicates, Virginia Woolf's *To the Lighthouse* (1927) can be seen as a First World War novel: though actual combat is barely mentioned in a few sentences, the whole novel is structured around the war's impact, as Chapter Two suggested. Woolf's *Mrs Dalloway* (1925) is in some ways similarly conditioned. A good deal of fiction in the forties – and sometimes in later decades – is likewise influenced fairly directly in structure and vision by the Second World War, even when apparently distanced from its immediate events. In fact, a feature of contemporary writing is the apparent wish – naturally enough – for some distance from immediate events. The shock of the war in life and the difficulty of communicating it in fiction encouraged writers, if not to avoid it altogether, at least to approach it obliquely rather than directly – perhaps a reason for the rarity of the kind of narrowly defined war novel Anthony Burgess identifies. In its title and its story of a flight from the war into a countryside familiar from childhood, P.H. Newby's *The Retreat* shares in a wider movement in the fiction of the period – one also apparent in the work of contemporary painters and poets, who often turned away from the war to pastoral or rural subjects. Dylan Thomas, for example, often turns back at this time to celebrate the idyllic innocence of a rural childhood. This movement is also identified in contemporary comments by P.H.

Newby and by Rosamond Lehmann, who helps explain the apparent absence of a 'great novel' specifically concerned with the war when she remarks that

> For the present most novelists are likely to turn back to the time when, the place where they knew where they were – where their imaginations can expand and construct among remembered scenes and established symbols . . . They will look to their youth . . . or they will invent allegories and fantasies.

P.H. Newby likewise comments of the war years that

> for most people who were beginning to write at the time experience could be divided into two halves: childhood and adolescence on the one hand and war on the other. Unless one wandered off into fantasy or allegory these were the inescapable themes and of the two childhood probably proved the more attractive.[6]

As Newby suggests, during the war and the years which followed, childhood and youth (to be discussed next) provided probably the more attractive or 'inescapable' theme, but it was also an unusually fruitful period for fantasy. As in the thirties, however, fantasy was rarely a means only of 'wandering off' from immediate events. As both Lehmann and Newby indicate, fantasy appeared along with allegory, often being used to provide contexts in which contemporary anxieties could be clearly and vividly examined. For example, in *Voyage to Venus* (1943) – a sequel to *Out of the Silent Planet* (1938) – C.S. Lewis is explicitly concerned with 'explanation of that fatal bent which is the main lesson of history' (p.8). As Lewis explains, his setting on a distant planet is merely a convenient device, helping the fiction to work as an allegory, showing in an earthling's confrontation with the Devil a struggle representative of conflicts with Adolf Hitler on Earth. Something of this struggle also extends into the last of Lewis's trilogy of interplanetary novels, *That Hideous Strength* (1945). In the view of some critics, it also influenced his friend J.R.R. Tolkien's trilogy *The Lord of the Rings* (1954–5). Some strong connections with recent history are suggested by Tolkien's epic tale of engagingly ordinary creatures from Middle Earth overcoming a malignant power in the east. Tolkien, however, denied any historical or allegorical significance for his work, and its major strengths are the straightforward ones often associated with children's fiction. A magical, alternative world; clear, exciting narrative; a fantastic landscape and fabulous creatures all added to Tolkien's enormous appeal in the 1960s.

In his trilogy *Titus Groan* (1946), *Gormenghast* (1950) and *Titus Alone* (1959) Mervyn Peake provides a vision less agreeable than Tolkien's, centred on the nightmare castle of Gormenghast – vast, dark, labyrinthine, and peopled by a cast of Dickensian eccentrics and grotesques. Their various evils and obsessive intrigues, their 'greed and cruelty and lust for power' (p.228) can be seen – as Anthony Burgess suggests – as 'an allegory of what had been happening in Europe during the time when Peake was writing the book',[7] his visit to the Nazi concentration camps in the wake of the liberating Allied armies contributing to the deadly stagnancy and gothic morbidity of his vision. The idiosyncrasy of Peake's imagination, however – its sour darkness and vivid pictorial inventiveness – make him virtually a unique figure in English fiction, and Gormenghast itself a creation sufficiently weird and self-contained to be at least partly detached from contemporary reality and history. Similarly, Wyndham Lewis's fantasies *Monstre Gai* (1955) and *Malign Fiesta* (1955) are partly independent of contemporary concerns: they are concluding parts of a trilogy, *The Human Age*, begun as long before as 1928, in *The Childermass* – a satire aimed at the whole intellectual climate in which modernism thrived, and in particular at the work of James Joyce and Gertrude Stein. Yet at a level of allegory both novels also engage with contemporary history, generally and specifically. Set in a kind of limbo of dead souls, each reflects some of the general gloom and morbidity of post-war life. *Monstre Gai* also contains a fantasy version of the Blitz, references to fascism, and a comparison of Hitler with Lucifer; while *Malign Fiesta* shows the Devil employing the methods of the concentration camps and expressing an admiring interest in the earthly invention of nuclear weapons – 'a technological magic,' he remarks, 'which may in the end equal us in resource' (p.62).

Like fantasy, the 'inescapable theme' of childhood and youth might seem a means of avoiding the stresses of contemporary life, but actually has a more complex and often less escapist role.

Wartime and post-war fiction certainly shows escape towards childhood security and innocence as desirable – but also, generally, impossible. In *Coming up for Air* (1939), Orwell's narrator George Bowling tries to escape the shadow of the impending Second World War by revisiting the countryside of his Edwardian childhood not only in memory but in actuality, but he finds that it has been almost completely destroyed by the effects of the First World War and the spreading urbanisation of the years which followed. Rosamond Lehmann records the origin of *The Ballad and the Source* (1944) in memories of her own childhood, but the novel looks back not so much on innocence as on its vulnerability in an adult world. Complexly structured, *The Ballad and the Source* traces the confusing, ever-expanding consequences of an original adultery upon subsequent genera-tions: children are among the narrators whose various versions of these consequences are recorded, their perspectives sharply focusing – like some of Elizabeth Bowen's fiction in the thirties – on the ways childhood can be shaped and darkened by the inadequacies of adults.

In his *Eustace and Hilda* trilogy (1944–7), L.P. Hartley similarly traces the sombre emotional consequences in later life of events and relationships in childhood. The trilogy opens with the fatal encounter of a shrimp and an anemone in a rock pool, witnessed by Eustace and Hilda during their Edwardian childhood and a symbol of the intense, destructive relations which prevail between them. These condition Eustace's some-times painful, disillusioning experience of Oxford and Venice between the wars and lead fairly directly to his eventual death. Disillusionment and loss of innocence are more concisely focused in Hartley's best novel, *The Go-Between* (1953), by his use of an ageing narrator, Leo Colston. His narrative retraces the emotional emptiness of his life to the shattering disillusion he experienced when he discovered, illicitly making love, two of the people he met during an idyllic holiday in 1900 and had made into 'the substance of [his] dreams . . . immortals, inheritors of the summer and of the coming glory of the twentieth century' (pp.19, 264).

At several other points in *The Go-Between*, Leo further outlines connections between his private disillusion and the 'failed glory' of the twentieth century as a whole. His remarks emphasise that childhood in contemporary fiction provides not a means of escaping history but, in Rosamond Lehmann's phrase, of 'coming to terms with the times'. Childhood innocence and its sad loss reduplicate the disparate 'halves' of life P.H. Newby mentions – memories of peace juxtaposed with actual experi- ence of the war – offering a context through which the wider disillusion of the twentieth century could be reflected within individual experience and examined in the novel. Other contemporary authors sometimes emphasise as explicitly as Hartley their use of contexts of disturbed individual experience to represent the wider history of the times. In P.H. Newby's *A Step to Silence*, Oliver connects his own early innocence with the naïvety of Neville Chamberlain's belief in peace, 'grieving' over the former Prime Minister 'as he grieved over his own past blindness . . . no one, not even those in the highest authority, was immune to innocence' (p.193). Elizabeth Bowen's heroine Stella in *The Heat of the Day* likewise reflects during the war that 'the fateful course of her fatalistic century seemed more and more her own: together had she and it arrived at the testing extremities' (p.134). Bowen adds of Stella and her lover that

> they were not alone . . . their time sat in the third place at their table. They were the creatures of history . . . of a nature possible in no other day – the day was inherent in the nature. (pp.194–5)

Joyce Cary also considered as 'creatures of history' the individual narrators of *Herself Surprised* (1941), *To be a Pilgrim* (1942), and *The Horse's Mouth* (1944) – a trilogy now usually published as *Triptych* – explaining that they all 'recall . . . the history of their times, as part of [their] own history'.[8] In *Triptych* as a whole, personal destinies are connected with historical developments throughout the period from the end of the Victorian era until around 1939, the outbreak of war more or less coinciding with the final collapse of the artist Gulley Jimson and his work at the end of *The Horse's Mouth*. The history of the times, however, is the particular concern of *To be a Pilgrim*. Its dying narrator, Tom Wilcher, obsessively juxtaposes past and present, seeking in the earlier life of his home, his family and the nation as a whole – especially its devastation in the First World War – the origin of factors which threaten a second war.

Wilcher's religious judgements about the operation of good and evil establish within this historical perspective the kind of strong interest in moral values which appears in various forms in Cary's writing throughout his career. The unusual strategy and structure of *Triptych*, however, communicates moral questions particularly forcefully. Each of Cary's narrators is involved in various relationships with the others, yet each has a radically different morality and world-view. The trilogy's three parts therefore express highly conflicting accounts of much the same set of characters and events, forcing the reader to arbitrate between very different yet wholly self-consistent sets of moral priorities. Each narrator's account is made completely convincing by the vitality of Cary's prose and the extraordinary variety of its styles. The three dramatic monologues in *Triptych* are each thoroughly unusual in vision – and distinctively imaginative visually – yet so different from each other as to be scarcely conceivable as the work of the same author. One of the most accomplished and original of twentieth-century novels, *Triptych* has rarely had the critical recognition it deserves, and Cary's career in general has been similarly underestimated. It includes an excellent early novel of empire, *Mister Johnson* (1939), and a later trilogy of similar structure and quality to *Triptych – Prisoner of Grace* (1952), *Except the Lord* (1953), *Not Honour More* (1955).

Cary's *Triptych* also helps to clarify a fundamental tendency in contemporary fiction. By considering an idyllic past not only as a contrast to a disturbed present, but as a likely source of its troubles, Cary shows a readiness to 'come to terms with the times' by moving through the anxieties of history towards myth. Like *To be a Pilgrim*, many of the novels considered above look back on a more innocent past not just as an escape from the war, nor only as a way of finding in personal life some analogy for its division of the century into distinct 'halves', but often to seek in earlier times a cause, origin or explanation for the disasters which so trouble the present. Rosamond Lehmann's title, *The Ballad and the Source*, and the novel's investigation of what 'poisons from what far-back brews went on corroding' (p.42) are paradigmatic of this tendency. *The Ballad and the Source, The Go-Between, Eustace and Hilda, The Retreat, Caught* and *To be a Pilgrim* all look back through extended personal and family histories – each partly representative of the wider movement of the century as a whole – not only to an idyllic past but to the emotional, sometimes sexual, complications which intruded to dislocate or destroy it. These recollections of an original misdemeanour and its consequences have some clear mythic parallels with the Biblical account of Adam and Eve's fall from grace and loss of paradise in Eden, a connection frequently made explicit in the novels concerned. In Cary's *The Horse's Mouth*, Gulley Jimson connects the story of paradise lost with his own loss of innocence in adolescence, and finds it an appropriate theme for his painting. In Newby's *A Step to Silence*, Oliver hears 'a sermon on the text out of Genesis' (p.209) immediately after learning of the naïve inadequacy of his own earlier innocence, while in *The Retreat* a character finds herself 'thinking of Eve and the Garden of Eden' as part of her regret for 'that state of grace before . . . the present' (pp.172, 171). The general significance of such regret for lost states of grace was emphasised by Henry Reed in his survey of contemporary fiction in 1946. In discussing its frequent interest in childhood and the past, Reed remarks that

> in a world of darkness we learn to hug that memory of comparative light . . . It is natural to turn and attempt to recapture and understand and detail that lost possibility of Eden.[9]

Attempts to recapture the past, regret for its loss or the loss of childhood, and nostalgia in general – all provide basic interests for fiction, and motives for its creation. As Reed suggests, however, such interests were especially focused by the darkness of the war years: what might otherwise have been personal nostalgia became around this time also historic. Middle-aged, and painfully aware of its many obvious ailments, in its forties the century itself looked back more and more often to the youth and promise of its Edwardian years, and their absolute loss in 1914. Novels such as *Coming up for Air*, *The Go-Between* or *To be a Pilgrim* – as much as or more than any in the 1920s – make of the Edwardian years a kind of lost Eden or Golden Age. Shortly after the Civil War in the seventeenth century, John Milton turned in *Paradise Lost* (1667) to the story of Eden partly as a vehicle or resolution for historical anxieties; for the sense expressed by his contemporary Andrew Marvell of the loss of a Britain once 'the garden of the world'.[10] During and after the

Second World War, the same myth appealed to authors trying to come to terms with the huge violence which had fallen like a primal curse on contemporary life, making that brief Edwardian era – before any major war blighted the twentieth century – so appealing. In this and other ways, Edenic retrospection offered a substitute for the 'familiar patterns' which, as suggested earlier, novelists may have found fractured by the war. Such retrospection brought all the power and resonance of myth to the contemporary imagination's struggle to structure and assimilate the challenges confronting it, becoming in consequence a distinctive feature, a new pattern, in the contemporary novel.

This pattern also figures strongly in Evelyn Waugh's novel of wartime, *Brideshead Revisited* (1945), part of a marked departure from the manner of his thirties satires. Like his friend Graham Greene, Waugh may have found the stresses of wartime making him more reliant on his Catholic faith: *Brideshead Revisited* is at any rate the first of his novels in which religion is extensively an issue. This is part of a new seriousness which contrasts with the frivolous satiric atmosphere of most of Waugh's earlier fiction. Few of his thirties characters are more substantial than Paul Pennyfeather in *Decline and Fall* (1928), a deliberately lightweight figure, as his name suggests, whose rapid movement through contemporary society is used to show the winds of change in the life of his time. Rather like his hero in *Sword of Honour*, Waugh remains aloof and ironically detached from this decadent modern society, generally withholding authorial judgement of it. Along with his insubstantial characterisation, this leaves a sense of emptiness and absence of values not only in the world presented, but also in the manner of its presentation. Highly coloured and caricaturing, Waugh's writing in the thirties novels such as *Vile Bodies* (1930) or *Black Mischief* (1932) presents animated surfaces with little more substance than cartoons – though they are sometimes as funny. Waugh is considered one of the most successful of twentieth-century humorists, rivalled only by P.G. Wodehouse, whose comedy depends much less than Waugh's on satire. Wodehouse relies instead on the consoling if improbable assumption that the English moneyed classes are made up of harmless buffoons, such as the pig-fancying Lord Emsworth in *Summer Lightning* (1929) and other novels set in the arcadian world of Blandings Castle. Wode-house's comic imagination also depends on the kind of plot – such as the inverted relationship of the foolish master Bertie Wooster and the wise servant Jeeves – successfully employed ever since the classical comedy of Plautus and Terence in ancient Rome.

Whereas the cartoon style of much of Waugh's thirties satire lacks the kind of depth which could fully engage readers' judgements or sympathies, a different manner begins to appear in *A Handful of Dust* (1934). The fuller characterisation and greater moral substance of its hero help to provide a touchstone for the soulless society he inhabits, and a firm focus for its threat to individual integrity. A similar figure appears in *Brideshead Revisited* in Waugh's first-person narrator Charles Ryder, who sustains within the society the novel presents the kind of moral values and commentary previously withheld from it. Ryder particularly emphasises regret for the loss of the serene, enduring life of English country houses, such as Brideshead, which the novel shows the war bringing to an end. Such feelings of regret for a lost, idealised life – and even Ryder's eccentric taste in art-objects – show *Brideshead Revisited* sharing in wartime fiction's Edenic retrospection. Looking back on Ryder's earliest memories of Brideshead as it was before the war, the idyllic second section of the novel is entitled 'Et in Arcadia Ego' ('I too was in Paradise'). The phrase reappears in a description of the 'decoration' Ryder keeps in his rooms at Oxford: 'a human skull . . . resting in a bowl of roses . . . It bore the motto "*Et in Arcadia Ego*" inscribed on its forehead' (p.43). Set in the fragmentary pastoral of the bowl of roses, Ryder's art-object provides an image of the distinctive effect of the war on contemporary imagination. The fear of death the skull repres-ents, and the desire or regret for lost paradises, are twin consequences of the pressures of war which are also thoroughly interconnected, inscribed upon each other just as firmly as the phrase is graven into the bone of Ryder's decorative *memento mori*.

As well as further illustrating effects of the war on the imagery and interests of contemporary fiction, *Brideshead Revisited* also exemplifies some of its consequences for the structure of the novel. Significantly, it is only around the time of the war, or in writing about it, that either Graham Greene, George Orwell, or Evelyn Waugh much departs from the straightforward chronology which is the usual structuring principle of their fiction. In *The End of the Affair*, Greene's narrator Bendrix constructs his story in a way which reflects both his nostalgia for the 'bright condemned pre-war summer' (p.25) in which his love affair began, and his resulting feeling that 'if I could have turned back time I think I would have done so' (p.66). In the novel's first section, each chapter opens with an account of Bendrix's painful life in the post-war period, then 'turns back time' to describe a part of the ended affair which some present event has brought back to mind. This sharply juxtaposes a disturbed present with earlier happiness the war helped to destroy: something similar is achieved by the structure of *Brideshead Revisited* as a whole. The novel begins with Ryder posted to Brideshead during dreary months of wartime training. On arrival he realises 'I have been here before' (p.23): his recollections then take the narrative back through his initially idyllic, later troubled experience of Brideshead, eventually moving on to catch up again with his present life in the war. Similar structures – moving from present to past and then back to the present again – appear in *The Go-Between*, *Coming up for Air*, *The Ballad and the Source*, and *To be a Pilgrim*. This kind of tripartite division has some affinities with Woolf's in *To the Lighthouse* (1927). At any rate, it shows the Second World War figuring in contemporary fiction as much the same sort of 'chasm' – the same kind of fracture in the normal flow of time – as the First had appeared to novelists in the twenties. Another new pattern found by contemporary writers to replace familiar ones fractured by the pressures of the age, it also once again demonstrates how history in the twentieth century inscribes itself in the novel at the level of form as much as of theme. Like Elizabeth Bowen's protagonists in *The Heat of the Day*, wartime authors were 'the creatures of history . . . of a nature possible in no other day' – 'the day inherent in the nature' of the form as well as the vision of the novels they wrote.

Malcolm Lowry's amalgamation of the distinctive form and vision of wartime writing along with techniques learned from modernism – rarely used elsewhere in forties fiction – helps to make *Under the Volcano* (1947) the outstanding novel of the decade. Typically, it opens with a chapter set after the outbreak of war – on the Day of the Dead in Mexico in 1939 – looking back on disastrous events in the past. Tracing these events – on the Day of the Dead a year previously – the rest of the novel shows the honorary consul Geoffrey Firmin doomed by insanely excessive drinking to a tragic downward course towards despair and death, despite full knowledge of what he is doing and of the chances for happiness he is destroying. His deliberate choice of a kind of damnation is highlighted at one point by his own reflections – after stepping over a snake in his once-beautiful garden – on 'the old legend of the Garden of Eden' (p.137). References also appear throughout the novel to a notice which Firmin translates to himself as 'You like this garden? Why is it yours? We evict those who destroy!' Lowry reproduces a final version of this warning on the last page of the novel, the use of nuclear weapons at the end of the war confirming for him, as he later explained, that the Consul's deliberate self-destructiveness was more than ever representative of 'the ultimate fate of mankind'. Throughout, however, as Lowry suggests,

> the drunkenness of the Consul is used on one plane to symbolise the universal drunkenness of mankind during the war, or during the period immediately preceding it.[11]

This wider symbolic dimension is emphasised throughout *Under the Volcano* by mention of the civil war in Spain, and the struggle against Mexican fascists, as well as by the discussion in the opening chapter of the war in Europe and many other details which indicate the 'drunkenness' of civilisation as a whole. More thoroughly and sadly than any of his contemporaries, Lowry represents in a doomed individual destiny the wider movement towards darkness and destruction of history in his time.

Lowry's technique makes this sombre vision especially compelling. While his *Ultramarine* (1933) resembled Joyce's *A Portrait of the Artist as a Young Man* (1916), *Under the Volcano* is similar to *Ulysses* (1922), both in its concentration almost entirely within a single day of Firmin's life – Lowry comparing the cumulative effect of the novel's twelve chapters to hearing 'a clock slowly striking midnight for Faust'[12] – and in the range of interior monologues and streams of consciousness employed to represent the minds of his characters. By refracting a strange, brilliant Mexican landscape through the 'whirling cerebral chaos' (p.309) of Firmin's increasingly drunken mind, Lowry challenges and disorients his readers more completely even than Henry Green, P.H. Newby or James Hanley. This communicates with exceptional force the expanding crises of the world envisaged. As Chapter Two explained, modernism has been criticised for its 'denial of history': in *Under the Volcano*, Lowry exploits and extends modernist technique to represent contemporary events and history – destinies public as well as private – with complete immediacy. This puts *Under the Volcano* as close to *Ulysses* in achievement – as well as structure and style – as any British novel published since.

Some of the anxieties which oppressed Lowry in *Under the Volcano* continued to figure in other fiction in the years after the war. The new threats of the nuclear age, for example, are cynically incorporated into the advertising of the bizarre Californian cemetery Evelyn Waugh satirises in *The Loved One* (1948). Whole novels are devoted to the subject. Aldous Huxley's *Ape and Essence* (1948); the popular novelist Nevil Shute's *On the Beach* (1957); L.P. Hartley's *Facial Justice* (1960); and John Bowen's *After the Rain* (1958) are all imaginative projections of the likely fate of mankind after nuclear disaster. In many other ways, as P.H. Newby suggested in 1951, 'the war seems, in spirit, to go on and on',[13] continuing to shape themes and patterns in fiction at least until the mid-fifties. William Plomer's *Museum Pieces* (1952), for example, is another novel of Edenic retrospection, with the Edwardian age once again figuring as a kind of paradise from which history has evicted later generations. Plomer's protagonists are genteel, bankrupt survivors of this age, aware of the anachronism of their styles and manners in later decades, and of the Second World War as the 'end of the world' (p.152) that had made them.

Museum Pieces shows the 'ineluctable shadow' of the war – and some of the patterns it created in the novel – surviving into the fifties. The war has of course remained for much longer a fruitful source of stories and settings for fiction. For example, in her six-novel sequence, beginning with *The Balkan Trilogy* (1960–5), Olivia Manning treats at length the events of the war and the years preceding it, using her hero Guy Pringle as a figure representative of British attitudes at the time. Guy is physically and in some ways metaphorically short-sighted: generous in spirit and faithful to the left-wing politics of the thirties, yet rather naïvely puzzled by 'fascist savagery . . . a new thing in the civilised world' (p.365). Its advancing threat forces Guy and his wife to flee to Athens (*Friends and Heroes*) from the doomed Bucharest shown in the first two volumes, *The Great Fortune* and *The Spoilt City*. Manning's detailed observation of this threatened city recalls Christopher Isherwood's *Goodbye to Berlin* (1939), though the greater extent of *The Balkan Trilogy* makes familiar a fuller, wider world, partly compensating for a lack of depth in individual characterisation. Some critics see *The Balkan Trilogy* as one of the best novels of the sixties: it is at any rate a successfully straightforward adult adventure story. This continues in *The Levant Trilogy* (1977–80), set at the time of the desert war, in Egypt, where the Pringles have fled from the continuing Nazi advance.

Two novels published at the start of the sixties examine the war and the spread of Nazism from the German rather than the British point of view. In *The Fox in the Attic* (1961), the first novel of his projected trilogy *The Human Predicament* – the only other completed volume, *The Wooden Shepherdess* (1973), is set on Hitler's 'night of the long knives' – Richard Hughes shows the origins of the Second World War in the problems and passions which beset Germany in the aftermath of the First. Such threats to European stability are sharply focused by Hughes's concentration on a hero whose naïvety and innocence make him unable to comprehend them for himself. Hughes remains best known for his first novel, *A High Wind in Jamaica* (1929), which enters unusually deeply into the vision and experience of children – shown to be alarmingly outwith the norms of adult conduct and moral judgement. The limited understanding of Hughes's hero in *The Fox in the Attic* leaves a similar absence of reliable judgement, forcing readers to assess for themselves the events – presented, Hughes claims in an afterword, with full historical accuracy – which moved Germany towards the Second World War.

Like *The Fox in the Attic*, Gabriel Fielding's *The Birthday King* (1962) locates the origins of the Second World War in the 'inflation, ignominy, and influenza' (p.18) which in Germany followed the First. Like Hughes, Fielding challenges the judgement of his readers by presenting the age's worst horrors – slave-labour, torture, concentration camps – without remark or censure. Instead, he shows them to be the cumulative, even natural result of the petty sins and connivances of a few conflicting characters involved in a family struggle for business power. This strategy helps to make accessible the kind of experience – the concentration camps in particular – sometimes thought beyond the scope of literary treatment. Even as the war itself has faded from immediate memory, the Nazi camps have remained as a besetting nightmare for later writing – a torment for the hero of Julian Mitchell's *The Undiscovered Country* (1968), for example, or for the character in Fay Weldon's *Down Among the Women* (1971) who talks of 'this year of Our Lord 1950, or rather P.B.5, which means Post Belsen Five' (p.21). Like Gabriel Fielding, D.M. Thomas finds in *The White Hotel* (1981) a particular strategy to communicate the shock of mass murder. The novel's various letters, case-histories, journals and Freudian analyses build up a highly complex picture of Thomas's heroine. Concentration on this single fascinating individual establishes some emotional basis for apprehension, or at least a reasoned incomprehension, of the enormity of her murder – by the Nazis at Babi Yar – alongside a quarter of a million other equally complex individuals.

The 'ineluctable shadow' of the war – and something of its patterning of writing – also appears in three novel-sequences begun around the time of its occurrence: the fifteen volumes of Henry Williamson's *A Chronicle of Ancient Sunlight* (1951–69); the twelve novels of Anthony Powell's *A Dance to the Music of Time* (1951–75), and C.P. Snow's eleven-volume *Strangers and Brothers* (1940–70). Complex, lengthy interconnections of individual destinies with the changing shapes of society and public life, each of these sagas can be seen as an attempt to come to terms with what the Second World War had helped make – in L.P. Hartley's words in *The Go-Between* – 'the most changeful half a century in history' (p.269). Only *A Chronicle of Ancient Sunlight*, however, much engages in the kind of Edenic retrospection discussed earlier. Rather like John Galsworthy in *The Forsyte Saga*, Henry Williamson traces in his early volumes – such as *The*

Dark Lantern (1951) – family life and the increasing conflict of spiritual and material values in London around the turn of the century. Williamson is still best known as the author of *Tarka the Otter* (1927), and *The Dark Lantern* is sensitive throughout to a threatened natural world, gradually overwhelmed by London's expanding suburbs. His writing is also prolific and evocative in period detail, giving a broad picture of 'vanished summers, of faraway sunlight and starry nights' (p.288); of a distant age, and of its hopes for a new century. These hopes are shown vanishing in several later volumes – *A Fox under my Cloak* (1955), *The Golden Virgin* (1957), *Love and the Loveless* (1958). Like the separate short novel *A Patriot's Progress* (1930), these reflect Williamson's own experience of the trenches in the First World War. His writing is probably at its best in these novels and the early part of *A Chronicle of Ancient Sunlight* generally; freer of the fascist sympathies which disfigured his later career and greatly diminished his critical and popular appeal.

Like Williamson's sequence, C.P. Snow's *Strangers and Brothers* incorporates many of the significant developments in a century of shifting values and pervasive violence – the disaffected aftermath of the First World War in *George Passant* (1940); the drift towards the Second in *The Light and the Dark* (1947) and *The Masters* (1951); the development of the atom bomb in *The New Men* (1954); shocking murder trials at the end of the sixties in *The Sleep of Reason* (1968). The centre of Snow's interest in all such affairs is defined by the catch-phrase his title *Corridors of Power* (1964) added to the language. The nature of public office, the exercise of power and its relation to private morality, ambition and responsibility are central concerns throughout the sequence. *Strangers and Brothers* is at its best when these issues are focused within a single firmly defined context, as they are by the setting of *The Masters* among a small cast of characters in a Cambridge college, their conflicts mimicking those of a wider world poised on the edge of war. In other volumes, Snow often explores public affairs more convincingly than private ones. *Strangers and Brothers* is narrated throughout by the lawyer Lewis Eliot: like any narrator, he is less able than an omniscient author to gain access to the private feelings of other characters. He sometimes also seems curiously detached – professionally remote – even from his own; too bland and equable to present compellingly the invention of nuclear warfare, for example, or the murders in *The Sleep of Reason*.

As in Snow's work, some sense of detachment and aloofness results from Anthony Powell's use of a narrator, Nicholas Jenkins, throughout *A Dance to the Music of Time*. This also appears in another way earlier in Powell's career, in the sharp, ironic authorial tones of thirties satires such as *Afternoon Men* (1931), following the example of Ronald Firbank in their use of understatement, implication and extended dialogue. Like Evelyn Waugh – also a follower of Firbank – in the thirties and later, Powell sets his novels among the moneyed, leisured, shallow upper classes. In *A Dance to the Music of Time*, Nicholas Jenkins's equanimity, restraint and fastidiousness make him an appropriate foil for this milieu – for the tortuous relations, freakish ambitions and unstable marriages whose unravelling and reforming occupy most of the sequence. Jenkins's qualities also particularly counterpoint him against the sequence's leading eccentric, Widmerpool, a character brash and awkward as his name. Widmerpool's unpredictable, bizarre reappearances help establish a kind of pattern and rhythm for *A Dance to the Music of Time* as a whole: Powell also relies heavily on social occasions, such as dances and dinner parties, to draw his characters together before they diverge again. Concentration on such social occasions – along with the use of a narrator who believes that 'human life is lived largely at surface level' (*A Buyer's Market*, p.27) – partly excludes deeper individual emotion, thought or passion from *A Dance to the Music of Time*. In its huge extent, however, it provides the most substantial anatomy of English society life and manners in the twentieth century. In particular, the gradual realisation of Widmerpool's ambition to claw his way up the social ladder, regardless of gentility or convention, offers 'a landmark in the general disintegration of society in its traditional form', as Powell calls it in *The Acceptance World* (p.128), which is a central issue throughout his sequence.

Snow's interest in public affairs, and Powell's in social movement – Widmerpool's in particular – show affinities with the writing of a new generation of novelists who began to appear in the mid-fifties and whose fiction Snow's work as a reviewer did much to promote. The Second World War continued to cast its ineluctable shadow over this and later decades (in ways further discussed in the next chapter), but by the mid-fifties it began to be clear that society had 'shaken itself' into the 'new shape' George Orwell predicted in 1940 would be necessary before a new literature could appear. This new shape – and some of the shaking – is reflected by the many novels in the fifties which examine new relations between social classes, and the opportunities for mobility within them, which had been brought about by the war's blow to tradition, the creation of the Welfare State just after it, and a wider spread of education, and of affluence, at the time. In title and plot, John Braine's *Room at the Top* (1957) and John Wain's *Hurry on Down* (1953) provide paradigms for this broad area of contemporary interest. Braine's hero Joe Lampton is as determined as Widmerpool to fight his way ever upwards to material success. After leaving university, Wain's protagonist shows his disdain for conventional social expectations by embarking on an equally determined descent of the social scale in a variety of unpromising jobs – a movement appropriately emphasised by the ladder he carries everywhere while employed as a window-cleaner. Just like Joe Lampton, however, he is secured in the end by a well-paid job and a match with a desirable, affluent woman. The same congenial destiny awaits another pseudo-rebel, Kingsley Amis's Jim Dixon in the social comedy *Lucky Jim* (1954). Showing heroes secured by money and matrimony, such endings exemplify these fifties novelists' disposition towards reconciliation with society, rather than the wish for its reform which they seemed to flirt with in their early fiction. This tendency is confirmed by their increasing (in Kingsley Amis's case, explicit) Conservatism once they became established figures themselves. Any anger in these Angry Young Men, as they came to be called, was largely self-indulgent rather than – as was sometimes supposed in the fifties – genuinely politically motivated.

Shallow or covertly conservative in its values, the fiction of the Angry Young Men was equally unadventurous in style. Its only real novelty was a sceptical, humorous, colloquial narrating tone: this was often learned from the example of William Cooper's influential *Scenes from Provincial Life* (1950), which also encouraged a distinctive contemporary movement away from metropolitan settings. Like many writers principally concerned with social change, Cooper had little interest in technical innovation, speaking for many fifties novelists when he expressed the view that 'the Experimental Novel had got to be brushed out of the way before we could get a proper hearing'. C.P. Snow likewise remarked in 1958 that many authors at the time had found that 'Joyce's way is at best a cul-de-sac'.[14] Like some of their predecessors in the thirties, fifties novelists' interest in contemporary society and change encouraged them to return to models modernism rejected, such as H.G. Wells and Arnold Bennett. The latter was particularly likely to appeal to writers such as Stan Barstow, in *A Kind of Loving* (1960), and Alan Sillitoe, in *Saturday Night and Sunday Morning* (1958), each portraying the Northern working class with a warmth and intimacy sometimes also close to the work of D.H. Lawrence. Like Lawrence, Sillitoe transcribes extensively the inner thoughts of his characters, creating an inwardness with working-class life which sets him apart from other writers at the time, making him one of the most worthwhile of the new novelists to emerge in the fifties. Colin MacInnes's 'London Novels' – *City of Spades* (1957), *Absolute Beginners* (1959), and *Mr Love and Justice* (1960) – show a similar intimacy with life in a metropolitan context, tracing like Patrick Hamilton in the thirties daily existence in the poorer, sometimes sleazy streets of a great city.

In general, however, concentration on the new shape society had shaken itself into by the mid-fifties did not establish the kind of 'major literature' George Orwell half-predicted might follow the war. On the contrary, some of the forties novels discussed above – Joyce Cary's, Malcolm Lowry's, and Henry Green's in particular – are among the best in the twentieth century; their themes, form and quality distinctively shaped and perhaps even strengthened by the challenge of the war, rather than destroyed by it as Orwell and other commentators feared. Much of the fifties seems drab by comparison: a period in which fiction and imagination were perhaps robbed of real challenges by post-war exhaustion, consensual politics, and the feeling the playwright John Osborne recorded in 1956 – that there were no 'good, brave causes left'.[15] Comments about the recent or imminent 'death of the novel' began to be made regularly by the end of the decade and continued for some time thereafter.

Fortunately, in the late fifties and sixties new initiatives and a recovery of some older ones quickly helped to re-establish for fiction at least a tentative vitality and diversity. This has lasted more or less until the present day.

FURTHER READING

Walter Allen *The Novel Today*, London: Longmans Green and Co. in association with the British Council, 1955.

James Gindin *Postwar British Fiction: New accents and attitudes*, Berkeley: University of California Press, 1962.

Alan Munton *English Fiction of the Second World War*, London: Faber and Faber, 1989.

P.H. Newby *The Novel 1945–1950*, London: Longmans Green and Co. in association with the British Council, 1951.

Rubin Rabinovitz *The Reaction against Experiment in the English Novel, 1950–1960*, New York: Columbia University Press, 1967.

Henry Reed *The Novel since 1939*, London: Longmans Green and Co. in association with the British Council, 1946.

Harry Ritchie *Success Stories: Literature and the media in England, 1950–1959*, London: Faber and Faber, 1988.

5 *Crossroads*

The Sixties to the Eighties

Several main strands of development can be seen contributing to the new energy and achievement of fiction since the fifties. Some of these – of particular significance in the last few years – are assessed in Chapter Six. This chapter considers the reshaping of the novel over the last few decades made by women writers; by various legacies of modernism; and by the combination of this rediscovered interest in experiment with some of the more traditional strengths of fiction. It begins, however, by considering the work of several writers – members of the older generation of British novelists in the late twentieth century – whose long careers span the years since the fifties and illustrate some of the interests and priorities of the period.

In several cases, these older writers were initially identified with the Angry Young Men of the fifties, but either moved quickly beyond their conservatism of form and outlook, or soon showed that identification with them had been wrong in the first place. The first case is illustrated by the work of David Storey, which shares some of the social realism of the fifties but is also informed by much deeper philosophical and other interests. The tough Northern setting of his first novel, *This Sporting Life* (1960) resembles Alan Sillitoe's in *Saturday Night and Sunday Morning* (1958), and Storey's highly characterised first-person narrative does bear some comparison with John Braine's in *Room at the Top* (1957). Storey's narrator, however, is a more complex figure, seduced by raw materialist ambitions and the symbols of

success, but also sceptical of them, and dimly aware of alternative priorities which he rarely finds it possible to act upon or
even to state clearly to himself. A similar division within the self
and in the novel's tactics appears in *Pasmore* (1972). This
connects fifties issues of class, materialism and social mobility
with deeper existential problems of identity, role and self. At a
realist level, Pasmore's ineluctable inertia and dreams of
blackness are simply the result of guilty recollection of his
father's work in the pits. They are also, however, figurations of
the kind of nothingness envisaged in the human condition by
the existentialist thinkers Jean-Paul Sartre and Albert Camus –
Pasmore particularly resembling the latter's *La Chute* (1956) –
whose influence reached Britain strongly from the late fifties
onwards. It is also reflected in Colin Wilson's *The Outsider* (1956)
and in Nigel Dennis's complex satirical fantasy *Cards of Identity*
(1955), for example.

William Golding's fiction began to appear at much the same
time as the work of the Angry Young Men, but contemporary
critical comparisons with them were never very plausible. Any
'anger' in Golding's fiction arises not from social conditions in
the fifties but – as he has often explained himself – from dark
conclusions about human nature in general based on the
experience of the Second World War. A scene at the start of
Darkness Visible (1979) shows very much the kind of 'ineluctable
shadow' which Chapter Four suggested the war left in later
fiction falling – both literally and metaphorically – on the central
figure of the novel. Golding introduces him as a child,
mysteriously walking out of the fiery heart of the London Blitz,
as if 'born from the sheer agony of a burning city' (p.20): one half
of his face is light, the other burned dark. Appropriately, he
enters upon a strange struggle between powers of good and
evil, half spiritual and half earthly.

The scene is emblematic of not only the source but the nature
of moral concerns which have remained fairly constant ever
since Golding's first novel – still his most popular – *Lord of the
Flies* (1954). This follows something of the pattern Chapter Four
outlined in war and post-war fiction – of general analogy with
the Biblical myth of paradise lost. But in demonstrating what
Lord of the Flies calls 'the end of innocence, the darkness of
man's heart' (p.223), Golding denies even the hope which

consoled many wartime authors – of positive values existing at least temporarily among children. The group of boys he shows abandoned on a paradisiacal island in the course of some future war quickly descend into savagery and devil-worship. Implicit comparison of their barbarism with the enterprising Victorian optimism of R.M. Ballantyne's *The Coral Island* (1857) – on which the story of *Lord of the Flies* is partly based – shows Golding's work reflecting a more general twentieth-century disillusion, accentuated by experience of the Second World War.

John Wain stressed Golding's distance from the interests of the Angry Young Men, his own included, when he suggested that Golding was more of an allegorist than a novelist.[1] As his comment suggests, Golding approaches moral issues not at a social but at a universal, allegoric level, often emphasised by settings remote in time and space from contemporary life: these appear not only in *Lord of the Flies* but in *The Inheritors* (1955) and *Pincher Martin* (1956). Some of Golding's later novels try to remain more firmly in touch with everyday contemporary life, but this can adjust awkwardly – as in *Darkness Visible* – with a continuing inclination towards abstraction and fable. In his later career, the particular strengths of his imagination may be best realised in the recent trilogy *Rites of Passage* (1980), *Close Quarters* (1987) and *Fire Down Below* (1989). Confinement to the perspective of an unreliable narrator forces readers to take responsibility for moral judgements which – typically of Golding's fiction – are at most implied rather than stated, and rarely show anything of the black-and-white clarity which might seem indicated by the opening of *Darkness Visible*. Confinement of the action to a ship taking emigrants to Australia provides the same kind of 'separate world, a universe in little' (p.191), as it is called in *Rites of Passage*, that Golding uses to focus the moral investigation of his earlier fiction, while also freeing his exceptional talent for sensual representation of the natural, physical world, the sea in particular. Descriptive powers of this kind, along with the range and challenge of his narrative forms, and his grave vision of the darkness of the heart, all show the affinity of Golding's work with the writing of Joseph Conrad. Such qualities help justify the award of the Nobel Prize Golding received in 1983.

In one obvious sense, Iris Murdoch was an even less plausible 'Angry Young Man' than William Golding. There are some ways, however, in which her first novel, *Under the Net* (1954), is close to contemporary fifties fiction. Its witty, colourful first-person narrative – in the voice of Jake Donaghue, 'a sort of professional Unauthorized Person' (p.140) – is not far from John Wain's style in *Hurry on Down* (1953). Jake's insouciant, sexy adventures on the edge of London's underworld also resemble J.P. Donleavy's *The Ginger Man* (1955), popular at the time more for its tales of Dublin bawdry and drunkenness than for its occasional Joycean vigour in language and technique.

Murdoch, however, is funnier than either Wain or Donleavy, and also more profound. As she has explained, *Under the Net* is indebted to Samuel Beckett and to some of the ideas of freedom and self-determination in the work of Jean-Paul Sartre. Murdoch was for many years a university teacher of philosophy, and her work, like Sartre's, is strongly shaped by philosophic interests. These include an idea of Simone Weil's – that morality is 'a matter of attention' – which reappears in various forms throughout Murdoch's fiction, and develops at several points into a strong moral concern with good and evil. This concern also shares something of the same source as William Golding's: Murdoch remarked in the sixties that 'two wars and the experience of Hitler' were still dominant influences on the life of the late twentieth century.[2] As she suggests, much recent fiction continues to concern itself with the century's wars and their legacy – Susan Hill in *Strange Meeting* (1971), Paul Bailey in *Old Soldiers* (1981), and J.L. Carr in *A Month in the Country* (1980), for example, all return to the First World War or its aftermath for their subjects. In Murdoch's own work the 'ineluctable shadow' of the Second World War and the continuing evil influence of the Nazis is particularly focused in *A Fairly Honourable Defeat* (1970) in the figure of Julius, an ex-inmate of Belsen who insouciantly destroys the lives of his acquaintances.

Yet while sharing something of Golding's concern with morality, Murdoch's fiction treats it in ways almost contrary to his use of fable and allegory. In *Under the Net*, Jake sums up the kind of morality Murdoch derives from Simone Weil when he remarks that 'all theorizing is flight. We must be ruled by the situation itself and this is unutterably particular' (p.82). This is a conclusion often illustrated in Murdoch's works by characters who achieve a balanced understanding of those around them by learning to give up distorting ideas or abstract concepts in favour of direct and true attention to each other. In another way, something of the same lesson is offered by the style of the novels themselves: by a dense, highly particular texture of everyday experience which resists the abstractions of allegory, or indeed the imposition of straightforward moral conclusions of any kind.

Some of Murdoch's novels do depart from this style, however. *A Severed Head* (1961), for example, occasionally demonstrates moral or psychological ideas at the expense of plausible character or action, illustrating an element of contrivance for which Murdoch has sometimes been criticised. Such criticism points to a problem or paradox perhaps inevitable in her role as a writer – committed, as an artist, to patterning and structuring experience in some of the ways her philosophy warns may warp and falsify reality. Several of her novels contain a self-conscious awareness of this problem, showing characters in flight from an enchanter – a god-like but wicked figure who imposes patterns on people and reduces them to puppets – who is also in some way an artist. This aspect of art is the particular concern of *The Sea, the Sea* (1978), narrated by a Prospero-figure who constantly questions the morality of imposing his visions and illusions on other individuals, or of shaping and rendering reality in words in his journal. *The Sea, the Sea* finds in this way a context in which Murdoch can directly confront and negotiate with some of the paradoxes in her own work. This makes for one of the subtlest and clearest treatments of issues of art, morality and philosophy which have now provided her fiction with powerful centres of interest for forty years.

The themes and style of Angus Wilson's early novels place him closer than any of the authors mentioned so far to the Angry Young Men. Like them, Wilson professed himself in the fifties 'against experiments in technique' and in favour of 'traditional, nineteenth-century forms' – particularly those of Zola, Dickens and George Eliot – through which he could realise his wish 'to convince the reader that he is seeing society as a whole'.[3] This impression is successfully conveyed in his second novel, *Anglo-Saxon Attitudes* (1956), by the use of a large number of coincidentally interconnected plots to illustrate 'complicated webs of muddled human activity' (p.290) in a wide range of social strata. *Late Call* (1964) is likewise a broad satire of the changing society of its time, reflecting the new rootless ambition and vacuous affluence of life in 'the nice neat England we've built' (p.157).

Late Call also emphasises the emptiness of this society contrastively, examining it in the light of the older, more secure values possessed by an ageing heroine, still able to return in memory to an idyllic childhood in 'the hot summer of 1911' (p.7). *Late Call* thus provides a late example of the kind of Edenic retrospection on the Edwardian period outlined in Chapter Four. This reappears at other stages of Wilson's writing. *Anglo-Saxon Attitudes* traces the consequences of a kind of original sin committed in 1912, also the date from which *No Laughing Matter* (1967) begins its extended history of six decades of middle-class family life. As in *Anglo-Saxon Attitudes*, in *No Laughing Matter* Wilson traces this life through a wide range of plots. By placing each of the family's six children in a different sphere of public affairs, he is able to provide a very broad picture of British life between 1912 and 1967. The great range of social, moral and political issues examined helps justify Malcolm Bradbury's suggestion that for many readers Wilson is 'the most developed and impressive novel-writer of his generation'.[4]

No Laughing Matter, however, is impressive in technical sophistication as well as social range. Substantial sections are in the form of dialogue, sometimes parodying the styles of Chekhov, Shaw or Ibsen; or of Joyce in the surreal 'Nighttown' section (Chapter 15) of *Ulysses*. Showing the six children looking at each other in fairground mirrors, the novel's opening provides an apt image for some of its other strategies throughout: much of the narrative is reflected or refracted through the highly individual minds of its protagonists, represented in a range of interior monologues or streams of thought. Wilson later admitted that Virginia Woolf – although he had initially rejected her example – eventually became the chief influence on his work. *No Laughing Matter* shows the extent to which, by the late sixties, he had come to rely on her styles of representing consciousness, and on some of the innovative energies of modernism more generally.

In this and other related ways, *No Laughing Matter* is a novel broadly indicative of the temper of its time. For example, by concluding his story with the emergence of a new generation of children – *habitués* of pot and the pill, rejecting in their turn the obsolete values of their elders – Wilson illustrates some of the new attitudes of 'the swinging sixties, the days of liberation' (p.55), as Margaret Drabble later described them in *The Ice Age* (1977). Whereas a new social mobility in the years after the war encouraged sociological interests in fifties fiction, and a mild anger at surviving social restraints, several factors fuelled a more genuine radicalism of outlook in the following decade. Resistance to the United States' war in Vietnam; the election of a Labour Government in 1964; the new rhythms of rock; eventually, echoes of the student-led revolution in Paris – all contributed to a new mobility of ideas and imagination, a rejection of conventions and a liberation of lifestyles during the sixties. Such new attitudes and energies naturally extended from contemporary life into art. Many novelists – even those like Angus Wilson who had once largely shared fifties priorities – rejected in their turn that decade's new conservatism and reluctance with experiment or innovation in form. Often, as in Wilson's case, this entailed a return to the examples of modernism; sometimes also – in ways considered later in this chapter – to new adaptations and extensions of modernist styles and structures. Another related area of development – and of particular contrast to the fifties – also shows how new attitudes, social and artistic, have continued to influence British fiction positively from the sixties down to the present day.

The fifties were rightly seen as a period largely of Angry Young *Men*: though both Iris Murdoch and Doris Lessing were sometimes bizarrely co-opted into this group by critics, its writing was largely male-dominated; sometimes, as in Kingsley Amis's sexist *Take a Girl Like You* (1960), offensively so. This changed in the sixties. In a decade which saw at last the unrestricted publication of D.H. Lawrence's *Lady Chatterley's Lover* (1928), and the general availability of oral contraception, a major liberation was in attitudes to sex: one result was a new questioning of gender roles and conventions, further encouraged by the appearance of an increasingly organised Women's

Liberation movement towards the end of the decade, and by gradually expanding opportunities for women in education and employment. This new consciousness of the particularity of women's outlook and social role opened up new directions for women's writing, which has emerged as strongly – and more diversely – in the last decades of the twentieth century as it did in the modernist age.

In some ways, the two periods are comparable, and even connected. Some of the innovations outlined in Chapter Two which became central to the modernist movement were made partly in response to women's changing roles early in the century, and have continued to appeal to women writers in its later years. As Chapter Three suggested, the kind of sensitive register for inner thoughts and feelings developed in the twenties by Virginia Woolf, Dorothy Richardson and May Sinclair was carried forward into the thirties by the work of Elizabeth Bowen and Rosamond Lehmann – and by Jean Rhys, who continued to exercise a particular influence in the sixties and later. Finding little to encourage her in the forties and fifties, Rhys ceased publishing novels and virtually vanished from public view, but she reappeared strongly with *Wide Sargasso Sea* (1965). This reconsiders the early life in the West Indies of the first Mrs Rochester – the mad wife who appears in Charlotte Brontë's *Jane Eyre* (1847) – showing her sensitivity recoiling and collapsing in the face of perverse harshness in her experience in general, and her new husband in particular. Rhys thought the novel's success had come too late to help her own career: its re-creation of interest in her work as a whole – and subsequent reissues of her earlier novels – nevertheless carried forward into the sixties an influential example of techniques established by modernism and particularly adapted to the presentation of women's consciousnesses and inner lives. To varying extents, such techniques have continued to interest several of the writers mentioned below, such as Anita Brookner. Another example is Eva Figes – also the author of an influential feminist statement, *Patriarchal Attitudes* (1970) – who returns directly to the example of modernism, writing in *Waking* (1981) a novel close to Virginia Woolf's *The Waves* (1931) both in structure – it records seven separate moments of waking consciousness – and in the reflective style used to record them. Such experimental tactics and general indebtedness to Woolf reflect Figes's wish to 'shake off the shackles' of 'the social realist tradition of the nineteenth century'.[5]

Some distance from social realist tradition is also apparent in Edna O'Brien's fiction in the sixties. In *Casualties of Peace* (1966), for example, the short, telegrammatic sentences she employs to record her heroine's thoughts suggest some Joycean influence from her Irish background. The troubled, disconnected quality of the thoughts themselves is also typical of her representation of women who are either lonely prisoners of their independence, or else victims of a wretched thraldom to men. Many of her characters share the kind of uncertainty Figes's heroine expresses in *Waking* about 'whether a good life was possible, by which we meant love, relationships with men' (p.71). Despite this underlying sense of doubt, rapid pace and sharp humour help ensure a wide appeal for her fiction. Reflecting some of the more liberated attitudes of the sixties, a mildly sensational explicitness about women's sexual desires – more apparent in her early fiction – also contributed to its popularity at the time.

The need for further liberation for women is communicated particularly forcibly in Fay Weldon's writing. What Emma Tennant calls 'the trembling sensitivity of Jean Rhys'[6] is generally given up in favour of reflecting a new firmness and determination in women's attitudes by the end of the 1960s. *Down Among the Women* (1971), for example, concentrates on straightforward emphasis of the awfulness of lives at the end of which women may have 'cooked a hundred thousand meals, swept a million floors, washed a billion dishes' (p.83). Weldon exemplifies this kind of servitude in the lives of three generations of women, tumbled from one representative situation to another to illustrate social processes and problems at work from the difficult days after the war until the more promising possibilities of women's liberation appeared in the sixties. Episodic and colloquial, Weldon's present-tense narrative is perfunctory in plausible characterisation, deliberately breaking the illusion of the fiction at the start of each chapter to emphasise as strongly as possible the political and sociological issues raised by her story.

Rather like Weldon in *Down Among the Women*, Margaret Drabble is less interested in the sensitive individual than in wider social questions, sharing the concern of her heroine in *The Millstone* (1965) with 'justice, guilt and innocence . . . sociological pity' (p.84). Such concerns make her much less sceptical of the social realist tradition than Eva Figes. Drabble is an admirer of Arnold Bennett, and shows in *The Ice Age*, for example, an ability like Bennett's, or like that of Charles Dickens, to represent the feelings of a whole society – to suggest, in this case, 'the spirit of the age . . . the state of the nation' (pp.34, 65) in the years of economic decline which followed the oil crisis in the seventies and doomed the 'days of liberation' of the previous decade'. Drabble has explained that her urge to examine general issues in society and its systems of privilege leaves the question of 'justice for women', though a basic one, nevertheless only 'part of a whole'.[7] This order of priorities is also reflected in *The Millstone*. Like *The Ice Age*, *The Millstone* is critically observant of issues such as class distinction, poverty, and the failings of the National Health Service. It concentrates, however, not only on this public sphere but on the private experience of a heroine struggling against the problems of her society, and against many counter-attractions, in order to achieve a balanced independence for herself – eventually helped, to her surprise, as well as hampered by the unplanned arrival of a baby daughter.

Neither Margaret Drabble nor Fay Weldon seems much interested in modernist innovation or departure from realist tradition, yet in one novel at least, each of them illustrates a way concern with women's roles has continued to affect the style and structure of fiction since modernism. Weldon's *Down Among the Women* and Drabble's *The Waterfall* (1969) are each written partly in the first person and partly in the third, a dual perspective which follows from the kind of 'splitting off of consciousness' which appeared in women's writing in the modernist period. As Chapter Two suggested, writing by women was particularly attentive at that time to the 'room of one's own' offered by the private, subjective space of inner consciousness, yet nevertheless remained fully aware that society observed and evaluated women objectively, even as objects, in terms of dress and outward appearance. A resulting sense of self, simultaneously both subjective and objective, extends from modernists like

Woolf and Richardson into thirties writing such as Rosamond Lehmann's *The Weather in the Streets* (1936). It continues to appear in a number of ways in the work of Drabble and Weldon's contemporaries – often divided between 'the trembling sensitivity of Jean Rhys' and less inward treatments of character and the self.

In *Providence* (1982), for example, Anita Brookner sometimes explores her heroine Kitty's mind through first-person transcription of her thoughts: other phases of the novel employ an aloof, firmly objective narrative voice. Such contrasts between inner and outer vision partly correspond to divisions in the heroine herself: half-French and half-English, Kitty is torn between her emotions and the life of the intellect; between desire for a lover and a wish for autonomy; between an easy acceptance of conventional roles for women and a more exacting pursuit of independence. Emma Tennant's *The Bad Sister* (1978) similarly examines what it calls the 'double female self', and 'the inherent "splitness" of women' (pp.101, 137). Tennant's heroine Jane, however, experiences such splitness more sharply than Kitty, perhaps as a genuine schizophrenia, driving her into illusions beyond sanity. In following these experiences, Tennant's narrative is itself split between prosaic opening and closing sections written by an 'editor', and Jane's journal, which describes a life of crime, magic and demonic possession. *The Bad Sister* moves with great facility between realistic vision of women's roles in contemporary society and a dimension of dreams which – though obviously beyond this society – also functions as a fantastic enlargement of its problems and a means of satiric examination of them. Tennant's novel is in this way typical not only of a continuing splitness in women's writing, but of some of its recent movements towards fantasy. Sometimes, these simply offer an escape from male-dominated reality: more often, they are also a means of critically commenting on it, or of creating contexts in which gender roles and identities can be freely re-examined and explored. These are opportunities Jeanette Winterson takes up in *Sexing the Cherry* (1989): they are also strongly exploited by Angela Carter, reworking fairy tales from a feminist point of view in the short stories of *The Bloody Chamber* (1979), and following in the fantastic narrative of *The Infernal Desire Machines of Doctor*

Hoffman (1972) a heroine divided like Jane between 'a drab, colourless world' and 'the fragile marginalia of our dreams' (pp.14, 19).

Fantasy, realism, divided selves, and split narratives all figure in the work of the most wide-ranging of recent women writers, Doris Lessing. Like Brookner in *Providence*, in *The Summer before the Dark* (1973) Lessing moves between inner thoughts and a distant, objective perspective in order to highlight the conflict of her heroine's self-perception with the image she presents to the world. Whereas *The Summer before the Dark* remains largely realistic, at several other points of her career Lessing moves like Emma Tennant or Angela Carter towards fantasy. This tendency is apparent in her five-volume *Children of Violence* sequence. It begins with *Martha Quest* (1952), a realistic account of a heroine growing up in the sort of African colony where Lessing spent her own early years, and encountering the left-wing politics and troubled relations between black and white which have often concerned Lessing herself. By the end of the series, however, the realism of *Martha Quest* is replaced by the fantasy and apocalypse of *The Four-Gated City* (1969). This change of tactics shares in the movement among authors discussed earlier – such as Angus Wilson – beyond the social realism of the fifties and towards forms which sometimes modified or rejected conventional narrative. This rejection extends into Lessing's work in the eighties as a writer of space or science fiction in the *Canopus in Argos: Archives* (1979–83) series of novels – allegorical, mythic accounts of creatures whose manoeuvrings in the distant cosmos influence the unfolding of human fate.

Even before *The Four-Gated City*, however, Lessing had already – in the course of her outstanding novel, *The Golden Notebook* (1962) – appraised, tested, discussed and largely rejected conventional modes of narrative. As she explains, *The Golden Notebook* contains a conventional novel as a kind of skeleton, but also the notebooks kept by its central character, Anna Wulf, recording her diverse, divided activities and feelings as 'free woman', socialist, private being, and author. Anxiety about the last of these areas shapes much of *The Golden Notebook*, highlighted by a range of examples of how, especially for a woman writer, conventional literary strategies – even words themselves – can misrepresent reality, or fail to represent it at all. Such doubts about language and representation develop into a critique of the whole enterprise of writing, extended through reflections on the nature of fiction; commentary on the style of the notebooks themselves; fragmentary samples of unfinished short stories; synopses and reviews of novels; and extended collections of the newspaper headlines Anna at one point uses to paper the walls of her house. These newspaper records of 'war, murder, chaos, misery' further emphasise the fear 'of chaos, of formlessness – of breakdown' which is communicated by the novel's thoroughly fragmented form (pp.251, 7).

Contained within this splintered structure, copious references to a chaotic contemporary world help fulfil the wish Lessing stresses in her Preface – 'to give the ideological "feel" of our mid-century' as well as making a 'comment about the conventional novel' (pp.11, 14). Anxiety about the conventions of writing and representation are strongly integrated in *The Golden Notebook* with concern about the historical reality to be represented, and Lessing has rightly recorded her disappointment that the novel has so often been seen only as 'a tract about the sex war' (p.10). In Lessing's writing, as in Margaret Drabble's, 'the sex war' typically figures as only a single element within a range of political and other interests – though a crucial one, and often a particular focus for the others. This range and particularity of vision, along with constant self-consciousness about technique, make *The Golden Notebook* a kind of paradigm for the strengths of women's writing in the later twentieth century. As the work of Margaret Drabble and Fay Weldon also illustrates, this writing is, firstly, particularly equipped to examine and 'give the ideological feel' of contemporary society from a specific, often sceptical and satiric point of view – the kind of 'alien and critical' perspective Virginia Woolf considered especially available to women. Secondly, technical experiment and self-consciousness about writing in *The Golden Notebook* and the work of some of the other writers discussed above shows extending into later fiction the priority Dorothy Richardson expressed in *Pilgrimage* – that women must reject or reshape conventional narrative forms as part of their rejection of a conventionally allotted place in society, and in order to represent the particularity of their consciousnesses and point of view.

A range of recent women writers has continued to develop these two areas of particular strength and interest. Maureen Duffy, Penelope Mortimer, Rose Tremain, Penelope Lively and Penelope Fitzgerald might be thought to belong principally to the first, observing society and women's lives within it in relatively conventional, realistic fiction. The reshaping of narrative form figures as a greater interest in the work of Marina Warner, Maggie Gee, Zoe Fairbairns and Jeanette Winterson. In fact, since new visions and new forms of expression are inevitably interconnected, they appear jointly, with varying degrees of priority, in the work of all these women writers. Their fiction helps confirm the novelist Ian McEwan's recent conclusion that 'women writers seem best placed now to use the novel seriously to open out relatively unexplored areas of individual and social experience'.[8] A continuing, expanding interest in women's writing is further assured by the support of Virago Press and other recently established publishers. While helping to enlarge the audience for contemporary writers, these publishers have also re-created interest in good women novelists from earlier in the century – such as Antonia White, Rebecca West, Storm Jameson, Rose Macaulay, Stevie Smith and Barbara Pym.

Paradigmatic of the potentials of recent women's writing, *The Golden Notebook* also shares in the more general interest in innovation and experiment – mentioned earlier – which originated in the new liberal mood in Britain in the sixties. This renewed disposition towards experiment has continued as another significant factor in the development of the novel down to the present time. Like some of the interests of recent women's writing, the directions it has taken can be seen to follow on from the example of modernism in general: even, more specifically, from the three principal areas of innovation – in structure, transcription of inner consciousness, and self-awareness about art – outlined in Chapter Two. Each of these areas has continued to influence later writing, but they vary in the extent to which they have been taken further, or encouraged new forms of experiment in later generations of writers. Some of modernism's best acts were the easiest to follow, but for that very reason the least likely to encourage further experiment or adaptation. Stream of consciousness and other modernist techniques for 'looking within' have continued to offer a technical resource to later authors – in ways considered in discussing women's writing in the last section, for example. But they have only occasionally been put to distinctly new uses – by Malcolm Lowry in *Under the Volcano* (1947), for example, in transcribing the thoughts of a permanently drunk protagonist; or in the twilit states of mind communicated by Samuel Beckett's monologues in the trilogy *Molloy, Malone Dies, The Unnamable* (1950–2); or in the failing, geriatric consciousnesses B.S. Johnson presents in *House Mother Normal* (1971).

Modernism's interest in restructuring the novel is more generally and more obviously taken further by later writers. Concentration of narrative within single days of consciousness and the use of memory to escape from chronological order are tactics adapted and extended by many recent authors. William Golding practises in *Pincher Martin* (1956) a kind of extreme form of temporal abbreviation, confining the narrative not within a single day but a single instant of mind. In *The Alexandria Quartet* (1957–60), Lawrence Durrell extends in his own way what he calls in his prefatory note a 'challenge to the serial form of the conventional novel', offering three separate versions of the same set of events, each presented from a radically different perspective. While Durrell tells more or less the same story three times in *The Alexandria Quartet*, under the influence of experiments in French fiction – the *nouveau roman* of the fifties – Rayner Heppenstall presents two different periods of time simultaneously in *The Connecting Door* (1962) and tells two stories at once in *Two Moons* (1977). Comparable double narratives appear in Brigid Brophy's *In Transit* (1969), and in Alasdair Gray's *Lanark* (1981) – its individual books presented in the order 3, 1, 2, 4, with an Epilogue and an appropriately named Intercalendrical Zone appearing in the middle of the fourth book. Serial form is perhaps most radically undermined by B.S. Johnson, the most enthusiastically experimental of recent British writers. *Albert Angelo* (1964) has holes cut in its pages so that readers can see into the future, while his famous novel-in-a-box, *The Unfortunates* (1969), is made up of loose-leaf sheets, intended, as a note on the box explains, 'to be read in random order'.

Modernism's strongest influence on recent fiction, however, has not been in the areas of chronology, structure or transcription of consciousness. Instead, it has followed from the kind of self-conscious concern with art, writing, language and style which Chapter Two identified in modernist fiction, and showed developing progressively in James Joyce's writing – from *A Portrait of the Artist as a Young Man* (1916) towards the playful, self-referential 'autonomy of language' which Eugene Jolas found in *Finnegans Wake* (1939). Later commentators have suggested that this 'autonomy of language' helps make *Finnegans Wake* not only a kind of grand finale of modernist innovations, but also a redirection of some of their potential for the later twentieth century – a period in which the powers of journalism and the media, and increasing suspicion of all systems of representation, have made scrutiny of language's capacities especially appropriate. Ihab Hassan, for example, calls *Finnegans Wake* 'a "monstrous prophecy of our postmodernity" . . . both augur and theory of a certain kind of literature'.[9] As Hassan suggests, a number of later writers can be seen to fulfil the 'prophecy' of *Finnegans Wake*, helping in various ways to justify terms such as 'postmodernity' or 'postmodernism' now usually applied to a phase of continuing experiment, extending the innovations of modernism, particularly evident in literature and other arts since the sixties.

Two other Irish writers served as intermediaries between Joyce and these later developments. Acquainted with Joyce and his work throughout its progress, Samuel Beckett extends an autonomy of language into his trilogy *Molloy, Malone Dies, The Unnamable*, which as the Unnamable remarks 'all boils down to a question of words . . . all words, there's nothing else' (pp.308, 381). Each of Beckett's ageing narrators consoles and distracts himself from failing powers and the 'black void' (p.278) surrounding him by spinning endless stories; evasive artifices in words. Each, however, also discusses and demonstrates the inadequacy of the verbal medium he employs – the hopeless impossibility of language truly representing anything, even its own failures – and the frailty of imagination itself, unable to sustain for long a narrative separate from unutterably empty circumstances. Each narrator is also, progressively, revealed to be no more than a storytelling device, a persona created by a subsequent one. The hollow voices of all these substanceless narrators create a chain of evasions pointing ultimately towards the unnamable author and the depths of an impulse to articulate which can neither rest nor ever, given language's frailties and faults, consummate its desires. Language and narrative imagination thus become central subjects of the trilogy – inter-related with Beckett's questions of being and nothingness, of existence in a universe for which ultimate sense and meaning cannot be found or made. Beckett's stark treatment of such matters finds compelling expression for the sense of loss and loneliness in the mind of the late twentieth century. Constant, paradoxical humour – and a verbal grace which half-belies the trilogy's demonstration of language's frailties – help make his writing unique in the literature of this period.

Like Beckett, though more cheerfully, Flann O'Brien also follows in the wake of Joyce, whom the narrator in *At Swim-Two-Birds* (1939) finds 'indispensable . . . to an appreciation of the nature of contemporary literature' (p.11). The material of *Finnegans Wake* supposedly unfolds in the dreaming mind of a Dublin publican: *At Swim-Two-Birds* concerns a publican who employs his imagination altogether more systematically, keeping his fictional characters locked up in a hotel 'so that he can keep an eye on them and see that there is no boozing' (p.35). Unfortunately for his plans, they free themselves while he sleeps, take over the story themselves, and use it to take revenge for his previous despotic treatment. Rather like Beckett's trilogy, *At Swim-Two-Birds* becomes in this way a story about telling stories about storytelling. Extending the 'augury' of *Finnegans Wake*, each work is a postmodern paradigm, a further prophecy of the self-reflexive foregrounding of fiction-making, language and representation which has become the distinguishing characteristic of postmodernism.

This development, however, might hardly have been guessed at in 1939, when the first publication of *At Swim-Two Birds* aroused relatively little interest. As Chapter Three suggested, although the end of the thirties saw the publication of innovative novels by new writers such as Samuel Beckett, Jean Rhys, Malcolm Lowry, Lawrence Durrell and Flann O'Brien himself, the main impact of all these authors came later,

principally at the end of the fifties and in the sixties. Like Jean
Rhys, Flann O'Brien found a new, wider audience at this time.
At Swim-Two-Birds was successfully reissued in 1960, the year
after Beckett's trilogy first appeared complete in English; at the
same time as the last volumes of Lawrence Durrell's *The
Alexandria Quartet*, and a couple of years before *The Golden
Notebook*. All these novels helped initiate and direct the new
readiness for experiment which has developed since the sixties.
The Alexandria Quartet further illustrates the kind of self-reflexive
concern with art and storytelling which has become a frequent
feature of fiction since that time. While drifting among the exotic
human flotsam of Alexandria – a city of 'five races, five
languages, a dozen creeds' (p.17) – Durrell's leisured community of artists, writers and spies seems to find aesthetic discussion
almost its only distraction from the relationships of love, sex and
diplomacy which occupy the rest of the novel. Their analysis
and demonstration of aesthetic problems and paradoxes –
including ones affecting the text in which they figure – occur
quite often enough to justify Durrell's view that the novel 'is
only half secretly about art, the great subject of modern
artists'.[10] By also including in *The Alexandria Quartet* a range of
journals, author's notes and fragments of other novels, Durrell
further ensures that art and writing itself become issues as
central as they are for Doris Lessing in *The Golden Notebook*.

Discussion of writing and literature is equally central in the
fiction of B.S. Johnson, who records Joyce, Beckett and Flann
O'Brien as his main influences. Johnson emphatically explains to
readers of *Albert Angelo*, for example, that the story he is telling
is all lies, and appears in *Christie Malry's Own Double Entry* (1973)
to discuss with his hero the progress of events and the
limitations of the omniscient form of narrative in which he
appears. Commentaries of this sort on the novelist's own
practice and proceeding, or enactment in the text of problematic
relations between language, fiction and reality, also figure
significantly in the work of several other recent novelists. John
Berger's concern with political and social freedom in *G.* (1972)
informs an attempt to liberate the text from the constraints of
conventional narrative. Berger mixes fiction with documentary,
discusses his tactics with readers and – through the disconnected, inconclusive form of the text – forces upon them

responsibility for constructing political judgements for themselves. Under the influence of the *nouveau roman* – often concerned with the nature of language, imagination and their shaping of reality – Christine Brooke-Rose writes in *Thru* (1972) a multilingual, punning, playful novel, its inventive typographical layout establishing a great variety of linguistic patterns and methods of creating meaning. Like B.S. Johnson in *Christie Malry's Own Double Entry*, Alasdair Gray – or a version of him – turns up in the Epilogue of *Lanark* to discuss with his hero the progress of the story and its likely outcome. This Epilogue also provides a list of the experimental and other authors whose work Gray claims to have borrowed or plagiarised. His imitative, parodic appropriation of their forms and ideas suggests that – by the time *Lanark* was published in the early eighties – a widespread familiarity with the priorities of postmodernism existed among contemporary readers. One of the principal authors of the *nouveau roman*, Alain Robbe-Grillet, pointed out in the early sixties that, 'after Joyce' and other modernists,

> it seems that we are more and more moving towards an age of fiction in which the problems of writing will be lucidly envisaged by the novelist . . .
> Invention and imagination may finally become the subject of the book.[11]

The work of Alasdair Gray and the other novelists considered above suggests that at least in some areas of contemporary writing, the postmodernist age Robbe-Grillet predicted arrived some time ago.

Other authors – including some of the most successful of recent years – share at least some of its features and interests. One of these is Muriel Spark, who began writing in the fifties partly under the influence of the *nouveau roman*, and perhaps also of recent conversion to religion. Like William Golding, she is concerned with questions of good and evil: like Iris Murdoch, she often focuses this moral concern around the kind of control, god-like or otherwise, that can be exercised by characters over each other – or by authors in creating their fiction. Both within the life depicted in her novels, and in the way writing shapes it, author-ity is a recurrent concern in her work. In *The Comforters*

(1957), for example, the central character, Caroline, begins to feel an analogy between the relations of self to destiny and fictional character to author; suspecting – with justice – that someone on 'another plane of existence' is arranging her life into 'a convenient slick plot' (pp.63, 104). In a novel as objective and puzzling in tone as any *nouveau roman*, *The Driver's Seat* (1970), the heroine Lise follows Caroline's example in seeking a life independent of authorial control, installing herself as the driving force within the plot by attempting to take over complete responsibility for the circumstances in which she is murdered. Power and authority are also central issues in Spark's best-known novel, *The Prime of Miss Jean Brodie* (1961). Its central character is a teacher whose sinister, nearly total control over her pupils leads one of them to reflect that Miss Brodie 'thinks she is the God of Calvin, she sees the beginning and the end' (p.120). Like *The Driver's Seat*, *The Prime of Miss Jean Brodie* provides at many points anticipations of events later in the story, allowing readers to 'see the beginning and the end' more or less simultaneously, and to evaluate for themselves Brodie's determining effect on the subsequent course of her girls' lives. Typically of Spark's writing, unusual, innovative narrative tactics are used to direct attention upon moral and psychological issues.

John Fowles records in *The French Lieutenant's Woman* (1969) writing in 'the age of Alain Robbe-Grillet' and other 'theoreticians of the *nouveau roman*' (pp.85, 348). Like Spark's, his fiction is often concerned with the freedom, autonomy or control of its characters. Fowles's first novel, *The Magus* (1966), for example, follows a set of 'God-games' through which reality is greatly warped – rather as it is in *The Alexandria Quartet* – by art, disguise and illusion. Such issues – in particular, the nature and authority of the writer – are examined more explicitly in *The French Lieutenant's Woman*, Fowles's best-known novel. In discussing his own tactics, and looking back on the Victorian period in which his story is mostly set, Fowles remarks that

> the novelist is still a god . . . what has changed is that we are no longer the gods of the Victorian image, omniscient and decreeing; but in the new theological image, with freedom our first principle, not authority. (p.86)

Various pursuits of freedom shape both Fowles's story and his means of presenting it. *The French Lieutenant's Woman* follows the education of a hero who gradually moves beyond conventional Victorian assumptions about social, sexual and gender roles. Concurrently, Fowles attempts to liberate readers from their conventional judgements and expectations of fiction, forcing them to choose between three separately presented endings to the novel, and to deal throughout with explanations of its methods and insistence on the constructed, artificial quality of its story.

In all these ways, *The French Lieutenant's Woman* illustrates particularly clearly how new attitudes in the 1960s extended into the fiction of the period – a new sense of freedom from convention in lifestyles, sexual habits and gender roles reduplicated in departure from convention in the novel. As well as criticising and reshaping the conventions of earlier fiction, however, *The French Lieutenant's Woman* also profits from them. Much of the novel's popular appeal derives from Fowles's dexterity with a thoroughly conventional plot – a love-triangle with a long-deferred climax teasing his hero between the various allures of two contrasted women. Fowles is equally successful in re-creating some of the atmosphere, moral interest, and traditional realistic style of Victorian fiction, Thomas Hardy's perhaps particularly. *The French Lieutenant's Woman* thus shows in a single novel two quite divergent sets of priorities – a highly traditional form of fiction appearing within an innovative, postmodern investigation of writing, illusion and artifice. In this way, Fowles's novel is symptomatic not only of new attitudes to life and art, but of the general condition of contemporary writing David Lodge analysed a few years later in his essay 'The Novelist at the Crossroads' (1971). In Lodge's view, the main road of English fiction remains 'the realistic novel . . . coming down through the Victorians and Edwardians'. Since the modernist period, however, and in the light of some of the developments that have followed, there have been what he calls 'formidable discouragements to continuing serenely along the road of fictional realism'.[12] The work of the innovative, experimental writers considered above constitutes one such discouragement. As the next chapter will consider, postmodernism has often been seen as a feature of writing less firmly established in Britain than elsewhere. Nevertheless, it has developed at least sufficiently strongly to ensure that, since the sixties, not only the main road but some of the alternatives initiated by modernism have remained appealing, sometimes – as in *The French Lieutenant's Woman* – more or less simultaneously.

This kind of crossroads of possibilities is also discernible in the work of most of the distinguished older generation of recent novelists discussed earlier. In most cases, these writers have not stayed entirely on one road or the other throughout their careers, but either alternated between them or established new paths which mediate between directions suggested by each. Like Muriel Spark, William Golding remains concerned, traditionally enough, with issues of good and evil, yet examines them through the use of allegorical forms or innovative narrative tactics. Iris Murdoch's concept of 'attention' generally commits her to a form of detailed realism, yet in *The Black Prince* (1973) or *The Sea, the Sea* she also engages in a postmodern scrutiny of narrative artifice, language and representation. For much of his career Angus Wilson likewise remained realistically concerned with contemporary life and society, yet he deploys a thoroughly experimental, postmodernist range of forms in *No Laughing Matter* and in *The Old Men at the Zoo* (1961). Though in *The Golden Notebook* Doris Lessing is as committed as any novelist in the sixties to challenging convention and renegotiating relations between fiction and reality, some of her other writing is much more traditional, and she has spoken of finding 'the highest form of prose writing' in the nineteenth century, in 'the work of the great realists'.[13]

To this roll-call of novelists successfully straddling a crossroads of fictional styles there might be added the name of Anthony Burgess, who expresses in his own terms something of Lodge's vision of recent writing when he remarks that

> we must welcome experiment in the novel . . . but it would be a pity to throw overboard all that the novel has learned throughout the slow centuries of its development.[14]

Rather like Doris Lessing's, Burgess's early fiction is based colonial experience of his own, realistically reflected in his Malayan trilogy, *The Long Day Wanes* (1956–9). Fairly conventional tactics continue to shape much of his later writing, including, for the most part, his outstanding novel *Earthly Powers* (1980). Like Murdoch and Golding's work, *Earthly Powers* remains centrally concerned with the conflict of good and evil. Burgess shows these forces operating within a wide, detailed twentieth-century history, starting – like *No Laughing Matter* – before the First World War; later investigating the consequences for post-war morality of the actions of the Nazis and the depravities of their concentration camps.

In one of the most popular and unusual of his many novels, *A Clockwork Orange* (1962), Burgess offers a more concise treatment of the issues of good, evil, free will and moral choice that appear in *Earthly Powers* and often elsewhere in his fiction. The uniqueness of *A Clockwork Orange*, however, results not so much from its moral lesson as the means used to convey it. To make acceptable its main suggestion – that its teenage narrator and hero Alex's free choice of evil is preferable to the robotic, brainwashed good behaviour later imposed on him – the novel requires a certain distancing and stylisation of the 'ultra-violence' through which he demonstrates and celebrates his free will. This is established by the strange, fluent, vital teenage language – largely based on Russian vocabulary – which Alex uses to describe all his actions. Extended verbal inventiveness of this kind demonstrates Burgess's admiration for James Joyce's use of language – he has published two critical introductions to Joyce's work, as well as an abbreviated edition of *Finnegans Wake*. Traces of a self-reflexive, Joycean concern with artifice and language are also apparent at several other stages in his writing, even in *Earthly Powers*. Its narrator is an author, whose self-conscious awareness of the 'cunning' and 'contrivance' (p.7) he uses in telling his story inevitably raises many questions about what he calls 'the capacity of literature to cope with human reality' (p.634).

Naturally enough, such postmodern questions also interest Malcolm Bradbury and David Lodge himself: both are critics and university teachers of literature as well as novelists. The fiction of each shows, at least intermittently, some of the 'experimental directions' which, like Lodge, Bradbury considers increasingly amalgamated with 'realistic sources' in recent British writing.[15] Lodge's *The British Museum is Falling Down* (1965), for example, is compressed like *Ulysses* into a single day of narrative: an admiration for modernist writers is further demonstrated in the novel by a wide range of parodies of their styles. Bradbury likewise employs parody and pastiche extensively in *Rates of Exchange* (1983): its various tricks and allusions also show his interest in structuralist, formalist and other more recent literary theories. Lodge, however, reflects the main priorities of both authors when he suggests that – although as an academic he is 'inevitably self-conscious about matters of narrative technique' – it is essentially to 'a tradition of realistic fiction' that his work belongs.[16] He and Bradbury both profit from the example of fifties realist authors such as Kingsley Amis: like his *Lucky Jim* (1954), many of their novels have a university-campus setting, often used as a focus for a wider satire of contemporary life and society. Lodge's *Changing Places* (1975), like Bradbury's *Stepping Westward* (1965), contrasts British and American styles of life and learning; Bradbury's *The History Man* (1975) satirises some of the chic pretensions which occasionally disfigured the new visions and values of the late sixties and early seventies.

Variously identified by David Lodge, Malcolm Bradbury and Anthony Burgess, a crossroads of experiment and convention figures not only in the fiction of older, established writers such as William Golding, Iris Murdoch, Muriel Spark, John Fowles, Angus Wilson and Burgess himself. The work of new authors who came to prominence in the eighties has generally continued to be shaped by the same combinations of – or alternations between – tradition and innovation. As David Lodge suggested in 1991, it is possible to see 'the novelist still at the crossroads'.[17] Sometimes this is apparent in a range of diverse strategies employed in separate works throughout a career. J.G. Ballard, for example, moves between the realism of *Empire of the Sun* (1984) and the fantasy of *The Unlimited Dream Company* (1979), which is closer to the strange, dehumanised worlds which appear in his science fiction. Similarly, Brian Aldiss alternates with his regular production of science fiction both the *nouveau roman Report on Probability A* (1968) and realistic novels such as *Ruins* (1987).

Amalgamations of new and traditional tactics also appear with striking frequency within individual works. Julian Barnes's *Flaubert's Parrot* (1984), for example, is in one way a fairly realistic account of an ageing doctor's fascination for Flaubert, but Barnes also playfully abandons conventional narrative in favour of pseudo-biography, bestiary, a kind of dictionary, a series of intimate conversations with the reader, and a variety of other unusual devices. While providing what is more or less a love story in *Possession* (1990), A.S. Byatt employs a similarly wide range of forms, including fairy tale, journal, academic essay, and occasionally sections of poetry. While Julian Barnes parodies biography, Graham Swift includes in his story of love and murder in *Waterland* (1983) half of a history and geography lesson about the Fenlands in which the novel is set. A comparable doubleness of vision and style appears in Peter Ackroyd's story of detection and devil-worship, *Hawksmoor* (1986): alternate chapters are set in contemporary and in early eighteenth-century London, and each is written in the language and style of its period. Alasdair Gray's *Lanark* also shows a duality of styles and interests: dystopian fantasy appears alongside the postmodernist devices discussed earlier, but the novel is also in part a realistic portrait of the artist as a young Glaswegian.

Continuing to appear throughout contemporary fiction, a crossroads of styles and strategies also shapes the work of Martin Amis. He outlines his own version of it when he remarks

> I can imagine a novel that is as tricksy, as alienated and as writerly as those of, say, Robbe-Grillet while also providing the staid satis-factions of pace, plot and humour with which we associate, say, Jane Austen. In a way, I imagine that this is what I myself am trying to do.[18]

Much of Amis's writing successfully realises the potential he outlines. The *nouveau roman* and other experimental forms underlie the fractured time scheme and weird objectivity of *Other People* (1981), or the puzzles about the identity and morality of the narrator in *Money* (1984) and *London Fields* (1989). Yet each of these novels also remains firmly based in contemporary London, *Money* also taking in New York. They provide a picture of late twentieth-century urban life more pungent and sleazy than anything Jane Austen could have dreamed of and yet – rather like her work – largely realistic, satiric and witty in quality. It is this satiric quality, as much as his inventive narrative tactics, which makes Amis such a representative novelist of the eighties – of an era of Tory government which has consolidated the debilitating social and financial hierarchies which appear in *Money* and *London Fields*, while consigning many more citizens to the 'clinks and clinics and soup queues . . . hostels and borstals and homes' which provide the background of *Other People* (p.100). Amis is an especially sharp anatomist of what Malcolm Bradbury calls in *Rates of Exchange*

> a time of recession and unemployment, decay and deindustrialisation. The age of Sado-Monetarism . . . factories close . . . vandalism marks the spaces, graffiti the walls, where the council pulls down old substandard housing, to replace it with new substandard housing . . . rain falls over factories which stand empty with broken windows. (pp.20–2)

Many other contemporary novelists write against this kind of dreary background of late twentieth-century decay. It figures as a further stress within the bizarre states of mind outlined in the precise, elegant prose of Ian McEwan's early short stories, *First Love, Last Rites* (1975), and in his novel of childhood morbidity, *The Cement Garden* (1978). Rather like William Golding, throughout his early fiction McEwan is interested in childhood, adolescence and the forces of evil which threaten it: in *The Black Dogs* (1992) he goes on to examine evil, partly retraced to the influence of the Nazis, on a wider historical scale. Some of the strangeness – especially in sexual terms – of the experience he envisages leads to a distinctive, disturbing black humour. Perhaps as a kind of nervous response to contemporary life – to a world resistant to moral coherence or even understanding – this kind of humour also appears in the work of several writers mentioned earlier, such as Emma Tennant, Muriel Spark, or Fay Weldon. It is also characteristic of recent fiction by William Trevor and Beryl Bainbridge, who shows in *A Quiet Life* (1976) and *The Bottle Factory Outing* (1974) a kind of gothic darkness in, respectively, wartime and post-war Britain.

Rather like Samuel Beckett, these writers perhaps consider that although late twentieth-century life may seem desperate, it need not always be treated entirely seriously. Humour provides one alternative to the gloom of an ice age of recession and unemployment: in the other ways suggested, recent writers have avoided reduplicating in the quality of their fiction the depressed condition of the life they contemplate. As Chapter Three suggested, fruitful combinations of a strong realist tradition with the huge potential of modernism had been possible for writers ever since the end of the thirties, but were long deferred by the Second World War and the exhausted conservatism which followed in the fifties. Rediscovery in the sixties of experiment, innovation and the significance of modernism, however, once again opened up the novel form to change and the productive synthesis of styles. Since then, the kind of marriage of tradition and experiment envisaged by Lodge – or more recently Martin Amis – has placed the novel in what Malcolm Bradbury described in the early eighties as a situation of 'expansion and possibility'.[19] More recently still, developments in the eighties and nineties have highlighted the significance of a further, cosmopolitan set of possibilities, additional to the largely domestic relationships or marriages of styles considered above. The next chapter describes the appearance in recent fiction of this cosmopolitan carnival of diverse encounters and new promises.

FURTHER READING

Bernard Bergonzi *The Situation of the Novel*, London: Macmillan, 1979.

Malcolm Bradbury (ed.) *The Novel Today: Contemporary writers on modern fiction*, Glasgow: Fontana, 1977.

Malcolm Bradbury and David Palmer (eds.) *The Contemporary English Novel*, London: Arnold, 1979.

Anthony Burgess *The Novel Today*, London: Longmans, Green and Co. in association with the British Council, 1963.

Jay L. Halio *Dictionary of Literary Biography*, vol. 14, *British Novelists since 1960*, 2 vols., Detroit: Gale Research, 1983.

Ronald Hayman *The Novel Today 1967–75*, London: Longman in association with the British Council, 1976.

Frederick R. Karl *A Reader's Guide to the Contemporary English Novel*, London: Thames and Hudson, 1972.

Olga Kenyon *Women Novelists Today*, Hemel Hempstead: Harvester Wheatsheaf, 1988.

Alison Lee *Realism and Power: Postmodern British fiction*, London: Routledge, 1990.

David Lodge *The Novelist at the Crossroads and other Essays on Fiction and Criticism*, London: Routledge and Kegan Paul, 1971.

Alan Massie *The Novel Today: A critical guide to the British novel 1970–89*, London: Longman in association with the British Council, 1990.

Neil McEwan *The Survival of the Novel: British fiction in the later twentieth century*, London: Macmillan, 1981.

Michael Ratcliffe *The Novel Today*, London: Longmans, Green and Co. in association with the British Council, 1968.

6 *Margins and the Millennium*

Towards 2000

A study of twentieth-century fiction naturally enough ends up by returning to a factor considered at the beginning, in Chapter One – the British Empire and its influence on literature. Britain's major historical experience in the twentieth century, along with the two world wars, has been the final flourishing, later decline and eventual loss of the Empire. What effects has this had on literature later in the century? Several are suggested in this chapter. Perhaps the most obvious is that the disappearance of the Empire simply impoverished British fiction, robbing it of subjects and settings useful to many novelists earlier in the century. Rudyard Kipling, Joseph Conrad, E.M. Forster, Somerset Maugham, Joyce Cary, Graham Greene and several other writers mentioned earlier found in the Empire a variety of useful contexts and opportunities for their fiction. Characters in the colonies could be confronted by encounters with unfamiliar places and values, the dilemmas of government, or simply an exiled loneliness sharpening an anxious questioning of their own outlook and identity. Moreover, the Empire offered many writers not only challenging encounters with unfamiliar cultures, but an opportunity for distanced, objective scrutiny of their own. Graham Greene remarks of writing about London from the vantage-point of Sierra Leone, where he worked for British intelligence during the war, that 'it is often easier to describe something from a long way off'. Anthony Burgess likewise suggests that 'if you want to write about your own people, you've got to get away from them'.[1]

The disappearance of the Empire deprived novelists of certain opportunities: it also added to a wider sense of loss which appears here and there in recent fiction in a number of ways. The twentieth century has seen Britain decline from virtual world dominion to an eventual role as a minor ally of the United States and an ordinary – if wayward – member of the European Community. This change in Britain's world role may account for a diminished scale and confidence sometimes apparent in recent novels. Anthony Burgess complained in the early seventies that 'we can no longer expect the one big book' from British authors, but instead 'fragments of an individual vision in book after book'.[2] As he suggests, the 'big book' in the later twentieth century seems more often the work of United States novelists than British ones. The latter seem more often to work over limited, specific areas of experience, rather than attempting the kind of ambitious visions (not always any more effectively realised) which have appeared in the United States.

This study has shown at several points, however, that literature not only reflects but seeks to compensate for the problems and anguish of history, reshaping in imagination what is lost or intractable in fact. As the Introduction suggested, this kind of process is sometimes more evident in popular fiction, and indeed a likely source of its appeal. In this way, Britain's loss of the Empire and of a dominant world role can be seen to account for the enormous popular appeal of Ian Fleming's James Bond stories, starting with *Casino Royale* in 1953. Numerous film treatments have helped to make these among the most popular of narratives in Britain since the war, Bond offering a kind of myth or collective wish-fulfilment in which British dominion secretly continues in the shadow world of agents and espionage – one in which Bond enjoys a particularly cherished supremacy over counterparts from the United States, where of course the real world's military and political power now resides. Ian Fleming has continued to exercise some influence over other writers in the spy and thriller genres, though sometimes in a negative sense. John Le Carré has remarked that the light-weight, melodramatic quality of Fleming's fiction – along with the contrary example of Graham Greene – suggested to him an opportunity for spy stories in which fantasy is strongly tempered with realism. This appears in Le Carré's dark, fascinatingly complex accounts of the covert brutalities of the Cold War, such as *The Spy who Came in from the Cold* (1963) or *Smiley's People* (1980).

Other recent media successes – and to some extent the novels on which they are based – can also be seen to owe their popularity to nostalgia for vanished Empire and uneasiness with Britain's diminished world role. Popular eighties films such as *Gandhi* (1982), *Heat and Dust* (1982), and *A Passage to India* (1985) sometimes drew on a qualified regret for Britain's supposedly more splendid days as the ruler of India. This also figured in the television series *The Jewel in the Crown*, based on Paul Scott's *The Raj Quartet* (1966–75). A certain nostalgia is apparent in these novels even at the level of form, in Scott's distinctive reliance on retrospection. Various flashbacks illumine his account of India's progress towards independence, starting from the 'Quit India' riots of 1942 and tracing the violence and change which led to eventual retreat and partition of the country in 1947. Like many English novelists writing about India, Scott is often compared with E.M. Forster, though on the whole his view of the Empire is less critical. The liberal optimism and faith in relationships characteristic of Forster's early work does not extend into *A Passage to India* (1924), which shows a prejudiced, complacent British community irremediably separated in belief and temperament from the people it seeks to administer. Scott's fiction, on the other hand, portrays this community with some sympathy as well as scepticism, looking back more benignly on the work of imperial officials who are shown to be as often genuinely committed as corrupt.

Two of these figures reappear in Scott's *Staying On* (1977), which employs the same sort of narrative tactics as *The Raj Quartet*. Beginning with the death of one of the 'old school' of British, the novel moves freely between present and past in its characters' minds, assembling a nostalgic, often amusing picture of imperial and post-imperial life, and of the moment of transition between the two:

> the evening of August fourteen, Nineteen forty-seven . . . the flagpole lit with the Union Jack flying from it . . . God Save the King,

and . . . that terrible, lovely moment when the Jack was hauled
down inch by inch in utter, utter silence. (pp.170–1)

Contrasts of the imperial past with the new India also shape
Ruth Prawer Jhabvala's *Heat and Dust* (1975). Rather like Scott,
she relies on retrospection, showing a girl trying to discover the
historical truth about a distant relative's romance, years before,
while partly re-enacting its circumstances in her own life.
Similar contrasts of the present and the imperial past – in a
different area of the Empire, the kind of African colony which
survived as far as the 1960s – also appear in Julian Mitchell's *The
White Father* (1964). Its central figure returns to London after
years of 'serving a vanished ideal' in Africa to find much has
changed in what has become only 'poor little old Great Britain'
(pp.164, 152). By juxtaposing London and Africa in this way,
Mitchell emphasises a connection between Britain's dwindling
dominion in external affairs and a loss of direction and
confidence at home.

Not all recent novels of Empire are coloured even by the
limited nostalgia which appears in those discussed so far. J.G.
Farrell, for example, sets *The Siege of Krishnapur* (1973) at the time
of the Indian Mutiny of 1857 – a much more remote historical
period than appears in any of the fiction discussed above – and
neither regrets nor celebrates the past. Instead, he suggests how
the Empire's loss – prefigured in the Mutiny – was a consequence of ethics flawed even when it was at its height. Rather
like Joseph Conrad at the beginning of the century, Farrell
shows how any controlling ideals are inevitably overtaken by
the materialist, acquisitive processes which are the real basis of
the Empire – how displacement inevitably occurs between
things 'spiritual and practical . . . the spreading of the Gospel
on the one hand, the spreading of the railways on the other'
(p.55). Farrell's concern for authentic detail adds to the
persuasiveness with which these and other processes are traced
in *The Siege of Krishnapur*. He includes at the end of the novel a
note of source material researched for its writing: something of
this concern for historical accuracy also underlies his realistic
style, vividly descriptive of violent action and adventure.
Farrell, however, also exercises an appraisive, often very funny

irony, making *The Siege of Krishnapur* one of the most entertaining as well as historically responsible accounts of the British Empire. Farrell once referred to its decline as 'the really interesting thing that's happened in my lifetime':[3] this interest extends into *The Singapore Grip* (1978), set in the period of dwindling power in Malaysia just prior to that examined by Anthony Burgess in *The Long Day Wanes* (1956–9). The kind of complex, critical history of the Empire offered by Farrell also appears in Timothy Mo's *An Insular Possession* (1986). Inclusion of newspaper reports and contemporary journals alongside its fictional narrative contributes to the historical detail and comprehensiveness of Mo's account of the rise of Hong Kong, a colony even more conspicuously controlled by the kind of corrupt materialism exposed by Farrell.

Timothy Mo also illustrates a consequence of the British Empire likely to be more lasting and much more significant than its creation of new contexts for novelists earlier in the century. With an English mother and a Cantonese father, and as a resident of Hong Kong until he came to Britain at the age of ten, Mo is typical of the ways in which – as Anthony Burgess puts it – 'British colonialism . . . exported the English language, and a new kind of British novel has been the eventual flower of this transplanting'.[4] In recent decades there have been many signs that this kind of 'transplanting' – also apparent in the work of Ruth Prawer Jhabvala, who has German, Jewish, English and Indian elements in her family background – is growing increasingly frequent and fruitful. Evidence of this appears in the list of recent recipients of the Booker Prize, a useful – though not infallible – annual indication of the best non-United States fiction published in English. The 1980s began with its award to Bombay-born Salman Rushdie for *Midnight's Children* (1981); the 1990s with the success of *The Famished Road* (1991) by the Nigerian novelist Ben Okri, now living and working – like Rushdie – in Britain. Among prizewinners in the decade between, novelists originating outside Britain also figured significantly frequently – the New Zealander Keri Hulme for *The Bone People* (1985); the Australians Thomas Keneally, for *Schindler's Ark* (1982), and Peter Carey, for *Oscar and Lucinda* (1988); perhaps most intriguingly, Kazuo Ishiguro for *The Remains of the Day* (1989).

Ishiguro arrived in Britain from Japan at an early age, and favours English for his novels as a means of reaching a larger, world-wide audience. Like the work of many of the writers named above, his fiction nevertheless reflects something of its author's origins, at least in its early stages. *A Pale View of the Hills* (1982) and *An Artist of the Floating World* (1986) concern aspects of Japan's sometimes painful modern history, even seeming to resemble some Japanese art in the subtlety and minuteness of their style. *The Remains of the Day* marks a new departure in subject matter, using the narrative of an ageing English country-house butler to provide an extended historical vision of the evolution of British life and society in the latter part of the twentieth century. Ishiguro examines this material with a precision, detail and apparent familiarity which might in one way seem inaccessible even to a partial outsider to British social life. On the other hand, *The Remains of the Day* helps confirm the views of Anthony Burgess and Graham Greene, quoted earlier, about the benefits for analysis of any society of a certain distance from its subject. The complex ironies of the butler's narrative recall in this way another foreigner, Henry James, who provided early in the twentieth century equally detailed anatomies of societies not wholly his own, his distance from them adding to the acuteness and clarity of his analysis.

Some distance from English society also shapes the work of many other younger writers emerging in the eighties: Adam Zameenzad, for example, born in East Africa and brought up in Pakistan; or the Indian Anita Desai, or the West Indian Caryl Phillips – a vivid historian of slave experience in novels such as *Higher Ground* (1989) and *Cambridge* (1991). Alongside writers such as Ben Okri and Salman Rushdie, the emergence of this new generation suggests that Burgess's transplanting has now taken place on a scale sufficient to confirm Emma Tennant's judgement of recent writing: that

> most of the developments in fiction . . . that have been written in the English language are likely to have come out of Africa, or the West Indies, or India.[5]

Though particularly relevant to the eighties, Tennant's judgement was actually made in 1978: however much it has increased in extent and significance recently, the success of writers from former colonies is certainly not altogether new. The reputation of the Indian novelist R.K. Narayan, for example, dates from the thirties; the Nigerian Chinua Achebe began publishing in Britain in the fifties with *Things Fall Apart* (1958); and V.S. Naipaul around the same time, enjoying his greatest success with *A House for Mr Biswas* (1961). Like Naipaul, Wilson Harris is a long-standing immigrant to Britain, though from Guyana rather than Trinidad. His long career is one of the most impressive of recent novelists in English, showing in *Palace of the Peacocks* (1960) and the rest of his 'Guiana Quartet' an imagination powerful enough to work at the level of myth, yet idiosyncratic and supple enough to resist imposing mythic or other patterns too firmly upon the fickle, changing forms of life itself.

This substantial, recently much-expanded achievement by writers from abroad needs to be seen in the context of an even wider internationalism which, as the Introduction suggested, is a fundamental part of 'English' writing in the twentieth century. An indication of the real nature of 'Englishness' – or its absence – in twentieth-century fiction might even be offered by the following discussion of national identity in Olivia Manning's *The Balkan Trilogy* (1960–5):

> 'Thought you were English?'
> 'Certainly I am. Typical Englishman, you might say. Mother Irish.'
> 'And your father?'
> 'Russian. White Russian, of course.' (p.718)

Not much fiction has yet been written in Britain by Russians, white or otherwise, but the complex lineage of Olivia Manning's 'typically English' character is nevertheless also typical of many supposedly English authors in the twentieth century. Manning herself is half-Irish, and Joyce Cary, Elizabeth Bowen, Lawrence Durrell and Iris Murdoch all share in one way or another this Anglo-Irish background. George Orwell, Wyndham Lewis, Mervyn Peake, William Gerhardie and Jean Rhys were all born outside the British Isles and remained expatriates for at least part of their childhoods; Australian by origin, Christina Stead spent only part of her life in Britain, though – rather like Ishiguro – she provides an astute analysis of post-war society in

Cotter's England (1967). As Chapter Two suggested, conditions
of exile and expatriation affected nearly all modernist writers,
and often functioned as an incentive for their innovations in
fictional form. International influences, principally from Ireland,
France and the United States, have continued as equally
significant factors in postmodernist and other fiction in the past
two or three decades. As Chapter Five explained, Joyce's
innovations were carried forward towards a later age by two
other Irish writers, Flann O'Brien and Samuel Beckett – the latter
as much a French author as an Irish one, since he lived and
worked in Paris and from the early forties usually wrote in
French, translating into English only later. Chapter Five also
pointed out the influence in Britain in the fifties and sixties of
new French philosophies of existentialism, and the widespread
interest in the work of Alain Robbe-Grillet and the 'theoreticians
of the *nouveau roman'* among innovative novelists such as John
Fowles, Rayner Heppenstall, Christine Brooke-Rose, Muriel
Spark and Giles Gordon. Echoes and influences from the United
States are less marked than those from France and Ireland, but
do appear in several novels in the late sixties: in Andrew
Sinclair's road-novel *Gog* (1967); Thomas Hinde's spaced-out
metafiction *High* (1968); and the various combinations of
fantasy, realism and self-reflexiveness in Julian Mitchell's *The
Undiscovered Country* (1968) or David Caute's *The Occupation*
(1971).

Such extensive foreign fields of interest suggest a representative quality in the scene John Fowles records as the inspiration
for *The French Lieutenant's Woman* (1969) – the opening image of
his heroine standing on an extreme southerly edge of England,
staring across the Channel towards an absent lover. Her desires
might be taken as figurative of not only Fowles's feelings, but
those of many other recent English authors who have had to
look across the Channel – or the Irish Sea, or even the Atlantic –
for new forms or visions apparently less available within their
own shores. In some ways at least, this is a useful and accurate
picture. Most of the major initiatives for change and development in twentieth-century fiction can be seen to have originated
partly outwith England, suggesting a lack – or even a dislike – of
new imagination and energy within this domestic scene. It is
quite possible, in David Lodge's words, to see twentieth-century

literary history in terms of 'an incorrigibly insular England defending an obsolete realism against . . . life-giving invasions'.[6]

There may even be specific reasons why commitment to realism – obsolete or otherwise – remains particularly 'incorrigible' in England. Ishiguro's *The Remains of the Day* demonstrates the continuing influence – strengthened by Tory government in the eighties – of the peculiarly English obsessions with class, rank, and social status. However debilitating these may be for English life itself, a strong, surviving sense of social position and class division does in some ways offer a seductive promise to novelists, helping differentiate characters precisely and providing a firm framework for realistic reflection of their interactions with each other and with their communities. Though especially appealing at times such as the thirties and fifties, when social stress and change seemed particularly to demand analysis, this kind of framework can nevertheless restrict the novel in both subject and form. Continuing fascination with hierarchies and gradations in social life and manners – especially among authors less critically, objectively aware of them than Ishiguro – can diminish commitment to wider political or metaphysical concerns, and the development of the novel form which often accompanies their analysis. An interest in class, in other words – 'the British language', as one of William Golding's characters calls it in *Rites of Passage* (p.125) – sometimes supplants concern with the technique and language of fiction itself, contributing to the staid, conservative aspect for which English writing since modernism has often been criticised.

On the other hand, as Chapter Five suggested, however much this staid image might have been merited by the fifties, subsequent decades have done much to amend and improve it. However eagerly the fifties, or the thirties, looked back to Edwardian and Victorian models, other decades have been much less resistant to experiment and innovation. And although influences for change have often come from authors originating outwith mainland Britain – or at least strongly aware of other cultures – this need not be considered to have only negative implications. In one way, it does suggest a poverty of adventure or invention in the domestic context. But in another, openness to foreign influence can also be considered an enabling, even essential, condition for innovatory, experimental writing, modernist or postmodernist, not only in the British context but within any literature. Postmodernism, in particular, is now recognised as an international phenomenon not only in the sense that its characteristics appear in art world-wide, but in that many of them are actually fostered by increasing pluralism in cultural vision; an increasing internationalism of outlook in late twentieth-century life. No author aware of two or more literary traditions can remain unquestioningly content with the conventions of any one of them. Contact with another culture and literature helps create for writers a sense of the character and limitations of their own, encouraging the pursuit of alternatives and possibilities of innovation and change. For writers anywhere, awareness of languages and cultures other than their own therefore encourages the self-conscious questioning, reshaping and coalescence of forms characteristic of postmodernism. The kind of objectivity which Kazuo Ishiguro's foreignness contributes to his portrayal of British society, in other words, awareness of foreign cultures, adds to other authors' vision of the form and nature of writing itself.

In the sixties and seventies, innovative fiction reflecting this kind of dual or complex cultural awareness was mostly the work of novelists such as Muriel Spark, John Fowles or John Berger who happened for one reason or another – education or personal taste – to be aware of foreign literature or thought, often French. The eighties and early nineties, however, have seen a much more radical internationalism of outlook emerging in the work of authors – such as Salman Rushdie, Ishiguro, Ben Okri or Timothy Mo – for whom post-colonial or other conditions of origin create a more complex cultural identity and a deeper awareness of styles and possibilities from beyond as well as within their country of domicile. In Rushdie's own terms, all of these writers are 'migrants' – people 'in whose deepest selves strange fusions occur', and who 'must, of necessity, make a new imaginative relationship with the world'.[7] Such new fusions and relationships contribute to the novel a renewed vitality and disposition for change, experiment and progress. As Emma Tennant helps suggest, it is particularly *developments* in the novel genre which have resulted from various transplantings of the English language – and as

Anthony Burgess remarks, a new *kind* of novel which has been their eventual flower.

This is more clearly evident in the work of Okri and Rushdie than it is in Ishiguro's. Social concerns help to keep *The Remains of the Day*, formally, a relatively conventional work. Rushdie's *Midnight's Children*, on the other hand, is one of the first examples in English of the kind of imaginative developments in narrative made by South American novelists such as Gabriel García Márquez or Mario Vargas Llosa. Like such writers, often described as 'magic realists', Rushdie integrates episodes of magic, telepathy, fantasy and fable into what is in other ways a realistic enough account of the life and history of modern India. It begins by returning to Paul Scott's 'terrible, lovely moment' – or, as *Midnight's Children* calls it, 'the precise instant of India's arrival at independence' (p.9) on an August midnight of 1947. Precisely, magically, this coincides with the birth of Rushdie's central character and narrator, Saleem Sinai, who finds himself as a result a kind of spiritual representative of the progress of his nation as a whole – 'mysteriously handcuffed to history, [his] destinies indissolubly chained to those of [his] country' (p.9). The historical interests of his narrative are widened by flash-backs to earlier generations of his family, and by flashes forward to illumine many later evolutions of events. This historical dimension is also clarified in another way by Saleem's self-conscious, postmodernist discussion of the challenges and difficulties of telling his story. Constant emphasis of its artificiality, of the constructed quality of his fiction, helps to prevent his personal story distracting attention too far from the real political and historical forces which surround it and which it seeks to focus. Emphasis on artifice thus actually shares in the novel's 'urge to encapsulate the whole of reality' (p.75). This urge is also satisfied by Rushdie's huge range of narrative forms and magical freeness of invention: *Midnight's Children* is one of the most impressive and significant novels of the eighties.

Comparable tactics figure in Ben Okri's *The Famished Road*. At one level, it is a colourful, adventurous account of a Nigerian childhood, and of the country's progress towards independence, perverted by corrupt domestic politicians as well as by Western powers. But *The Famished Road* also shows this realistically described domain interfused with 'the songs and fragrances of another world, a world beyond death' (p.485) – a fantastic, visionary, spirit-world whose powers and influences Okri nevertheless records very simply and straightforwardly. Like *Midnight's Children*, *The Famished Road* shows with great conviction how 'hallucinations . . . stories and rumours . . . become some of the most extravagant realities of our lives' (p.37), and vice versa. Like Rushdie, Okri uses the vision and fragrance of magical, fantastic narrative to expand and illumine the realities of daily life and the political, historical forces which shape it – a fluent integration of magic and realism which shows him as aware as Rushdie of recent developments in fiction world-wide. The work of each author also confirms the potential, outlined above, of amending the practices of one literature or culture in the light of awareness of the demands and possibilities of another – Okri, like Chinua Achebe, using the vitality of Nigerian fable and folk-tale to reshape the conventions of the novel in English.

Writers such as Rushdie and Okri thus suggest a particular literary potential in post-colonial Britain, in which conflicting, increasingly plural cultural awarenesses encourage critical consciousness of the conventions of the novel, and a readiness to adapt them to new needs and pressures. This kind of promise is not confined to the work of recent immigrants such as Rushdie and Okri, but figures comparably in the work of many other twentieth-century novelists in English, part of an inter-nationalism which can be seen as the consequence of a longer history of English colonialism. Irish writers, for example, belong in a way to an older, longer-established layer of English empire. In Joyce's *A Portrait of the Artist as a Young Man* (1916), it is uneasiness with what is really the speech of a ruling power that Stephen Dedalus expresses when he meets an English priest and reflects that

> His language, so familiar and so foreign, will always be for me an acquired speech. I have not made or accepted its words. My voice holds them at bay. My soul frets in the shadow of his language. (p.189)

Chapter Two located some of Joyce's own disposition for experiment and innovation in this kind of uneasiness with words and language. Later Irish writers are likely to have been similarly disposed to escape the shadow of English language and culture by adapting its forms to their own needs, rather than accepting them unchallenged. The outstanding inventiveness of Irish fiction in the twentieth century may be the result of this urge. John Banville, Benedict Kiely, Bernard MacLaverty, Brian Moore and many other authors in the last decades of the century continue to demonstrate this strength in Irish writing and its continuing influence on fiction in English.

Other novelists, within mainland Britain, are likely to have experienced comparable feelings, particularly in recent years. While the affluent, Conservative-dominated South East grows increasingly apart from the rest of the country, yet retains control over the language and ideas of most of its media, a sense of cultural separateness and the need for separate forms are likely to result elsewhere. This is especially so in Scotland, where some desire for cultural, linguistic and political autonomy has always existed. Some of the Scottish authors already discussed – such as Alasdair Gray, Muriel Spark or Emma Tennant – give evidence of a readiness to evolve new forms which may result from Scotland's political situation and tensions between its literary traditions and English ones. Alasdair Gray's writing particularly illustrates ways a Scottish background can encourage experiment in directions which coincide with the new dispositions of a postmodern age, while also belonging to a longer history of Scottish writing. Gray's double allegiance to realism and fantasy in *Lanark* (1981) and in *1982, Janine* (1984) is typical not only of the recent postmodern crossroads of realist and alternative conventions outlined in Chapter Five. It also extends a tradition of split narratives and identities much longer apparent in Scottish fiction; perhaps best exemplified by R.L. Stevenson's study of the fantastic metamorphosis of an ordinary man in *Dr Jekyll and Mr Hyde* (1886). The doubleness in Stevenson's narrative and in the identity of its hero figure in their own way a simultaneous accommodation with and estrangement from official English language and culture – a version of the simultaneous familiarity and foreignness Stephen discusses in *A Portrait of the Artist as a Young Man*. Similar dividedness continues to appear in the narratives of Scottish novelists emerging in recent years – in the double vision of the self in Ron Butlin's *The Sound of my Voice* (1987); in the precarious identity of Brian McCabe's protagonist in *The Other McCoy* (1990); in the sometimes-split persona of the narrator in Andrew Greig's *Electric Brae* (1992); or in Ian Banks's complex mixtures of fantasy, hallucination and reality in *The Bridge* (1986).

The outstanding author of the later eighties, James Kelman, profits from a double allegiance of his own, to traditional and postmodern possibilities. This is evident in *A Disaffection* (1989), which won the James Tait Black Prize for fiction in 1990. In one way, Kelman's writing shares in a tradition of hard-worded urban realism which in the late twentieth century has appeared particularly in the work of West of Scotland writers such as Archie Hind, George Friel, Frederic Lindsay or William McIlvanney in *Laidlaw* (1977), for example. In tracing a Glasgow teacher's expanding uneasiness with his life and profession, however, *A Disaffection* also displays the kind of intense, minute attention to oppressed inner consciousness, and highly flexible transcription of an inner voice, which appears in the writing of Samuel Beckett, to whom Kelman is probably as close in quality and style as any recent novelist. In *Lanark*, Alasdair Gray describes Glasgow as 'the sort of industrial city where most people live nowadays but nobody imagines living' (p.105): this poverty in imagination is comprehensively redressed by the work of both Kelman and Gray – by Gray's highly diverse, imaginative visions of the city in *Lanark*; by Kelman's fluent elucidation, in *A Disaffection* and elsewhere, of the uneasy reflex of urban deprivation deep within the self.

With authors such as George Mackay Brown, William Boyd, Robin Jenkins and Ronald Frame continuing to write recently in more conventional idioms, and the emergence of other new novelists such as Alan Spence, Robert Alan Jamieson and Janice Galloway, Scottish fiction since the seventies has matched the success of the literary renaissance of the late twenties and thirties. A contributory factor in this achievement may have been the failure of the referendum on devolution in 1979. What history refuses, fiction and imagination reshape and express. A frustrated wish for political autonomy may have sublimated itself into a heightened sense of imaginative and cultural difference of the kind which – as this chapter has suggested throughout – encourages development of new styles and forms for the novel.

At any rate, Scottish writers – or those from other minority nationalities within the 'United' Kingdom – can be seen to share some of the experience of post-colonial immigrants, finding English culture both familiar yet significantly foreign; an acquired speech more likely to be adapted than uncritically adopted. To this set of writers 'fretting' against conventional forms there might be added another section of novelists, experiencing in their own way a sense of distance and partial exile from a society which nevertheless remains familiar as the context of their daily lives. This is much the feeling Virginia Woolf records in *A Room of One's Own* (1929) when she suggests that – rather than feeling a 'natural inheritor' of English civilisation – any woman is bound to be partly 'outside of it, alien and critical'.[8] As Chapter Five suggested, in recent years such 'alien and critical' attitudes have continued to contribute to sharp, particular visions of contemporary society, and have also been fruitfully applied to the novel form itself, encouraging innovation and change. Women writers such as Emma Tennant, Angela Carter and Jeanette Winterson have also shown themselves at least as alert as Rushdie to the potential of magic realist styles. The complex, highly various forms employed by A.S. Byatt in *Possession* – a Booker Prize winner in 1990 – further confirm the continuing importance of experiment and diversity among women writers.

The work of these writers and of those from national and post-colonial minorities suggests that the strongest achievements of recent fiction have come from areas belonging in one way or another to the margins rather than the mainstream of influence in British society. Peripheries of political power and influence seem more and more often to offer the best openings towards the centres of literary success. Though this might seem paradoxical, there are good reasons why it should be so, some suggested above: these are also supported by the views of one of the most influential of narrative theorists, Mikhail Bakhtin. Bakhtin suggests that competing cultural strata, voices and languages are fundamental to the nature and constitution of the novel – essentially 'a *system* of languages that mutually and ideologically interanimate each other'.[9] This constitution he sees as retraceable, by analogy at least, to the parodic and subversive practices – the mockeries as well as celebrations of mainstream, official culture – of carnival in the middle ages. These carnival-esque qualities are more or less present within any society, and any novel, but may be particularly focused by the situation of late twentieth-century Britain. However much it suffers in actuality – economically and socially – from the age of Sado-Monetarism Malcolm Bradbury and other authors have satirised, post-colonial Britain is increasingly, in the terms Bakhtin outlines, a carnival of diverse linguistic, cultural and racial possibilities.

This context – in which marginal influences compete with or contribute to the mainstream, and conventions survive or are subverted by innovative alternatives – ought to prove a fruitful one for writing in Britain as the millennium approaches. The realist traditions which have remained a strong force in British writing throughout the century will no doubt retain their influence until its end. Yet the range of alternatives has expanded far enough to suggest that David Lodge's metaphor of the crossroads may soon seem inadequate – an image from an age of greater simplicity in literary route-planning. Traffic in Britain has moved beyond the crossroads to the spaghetti junction: its complexity – and faintly foreign resonance – may make it a better metaphor for an era of writing in which long-serving main roads remain discernible, but are increasingly overwhelmed by new directions, recombining and diversifying the old.

Of course this diversity of possibilities is not unique to writing in Britain, only one of several countries to have experienced the loss of an empire in the later twentieth century, and in some ways more resistant than others to the internationalism of contemporary life. Even the internal stresses of a 'united' kingdom are shared in one way or another by several other European countries. If there is any uniqueness to Britain's position at the end of the twentieth century, it is in consequence of the increasing role of English as an international language. The world the Empire vacated is still occupied by the language that it used. As a result, it may be that many more writers of the vision and vitality of Ishiguro, Rushdie and others mentioned in this chapter will continue to write in English and work in Britain, perhaps making the last part of this century and the beginning of the next – like the late nineteenth and early twentieth centuries – a particularly interesting one for literature. Writing in that early part of the twentieth century, in the modernist period, Virginia Woolf concluded her essay 'Mr. Bennett and Mrs. Brown' – after insisting throughout on the desirability of change and development – by making 'a surpassingly rash prediction . . . [that] we are trembling on the verge of one of the great ages of English literature'.[10] Perhaps it is presumptuous enough for the present study to have surveyed a whole century's fiction in six short chapters without it indulging in Woolf's penchant for predicting the future as well. And it would certainly be rash – especially at a time when it is so hard for writers and publishers to survive financially in Britain – to proclaim an approaching great age of literature with much conviction. Nevertheless, there are reasons for some optimism about the vitality of the novel in Britain over the next few years – though its best achievements will most likely be the work of 'Englishmen' (if the work of men at all) typical only of the kind of 'strange fusions' Olivia Manning and Salman Rushdie outline.

FURTHER READING

Bill Ashcroft, Gareth Griffiths and Helen Tiffin *The Empire Writes Back: Theory and practice in post-colonial literature*, London: Routledge, 1989.

Martin Green *The English Novel in the Twentieth Century: The doom of empire*, London: Routledge and Kegan Paul, 1984.

Jeffrey Meyers *Fiction and the Colonial Experience*, Ipswich: Boydell Press, 1973.

Dennis Walder (ed.) *Literature in the Modern World: Critical essays and documents*, Oxford: Oxford University Press, 1990, especially Part II v & vi.

Gavin Wallace and Randall Stevenson (eds.) *The Scottish Novel since the Seventies: New visions, old dreams*, Edinburgh: Edinburgh University Press, 1993.

Notes

INTRODUCTION

1. See Walter Allen, *The English Novel: A short critical history* (London: Phoenix House, 1954), pp.250–1; and Peter Keating, *The Haunted Study: A social history of the English novel 1875–1914* (London: Secker and Warburg, 1989), especially Parts One and Four.
2. Virginia Woolf, 'Modern Fiction' (1919), rpt. in *Collected Essays* (London: Hogarth Press, 1966), vol. II, p.103.

CHAPTER ONE

1. Arthur Conan Doyle, *The Great Boer War* (London: Thomas Nelson, 1903), pp.15, 551.
2. H.G. Wells, 'The Contemporary Novel' (1911), rpt. in Leon Edel and Gordon N. Ray (eds.), *Henry James and H.G. Wells* (London: Rupert Hart-Davis, 1958), p.147.
3. Conan Doyle, *The Great Boer War* (see note 1), p.152.
4. H.G. Wells, letter to Henry James, 8 July 1915, rpt. in Edel and Ray, *Henry James and H.G. Wells* (see note 2), p.264.
5. Virginia Woolf, 'Mr. Bennett and Mrs. Brown' (1924), rpt. in *Collected Essays* (London: Hogarth Press, 1966), vol. I, pp.320, 321.
6. *ibid.*, p.326.
7. D.H. Lawrence, 'John Galsworthy' (1928), rpt. in Anthony Beal (ed.), *Selected Literary Criticism* (London: Heinemann, 1955), pp.123, 120.

8. Henry James, 'The Younger Generation' (1914), rpt. in Edel and Ray, *Henry James and H.G. Wells* (see note 2), pp.187–8.

9. *ibid.*, pp.196, 195; Henry James, Prefaces to *The Spoils of Poynton*, *The Tragic Muse* and *The Princess Casamassima*, rpt. in R.P. Blackmur (ed.), *The Art of the Novel: Critical prefaces* (London: Charles Scribner's Sons, 1934), pp.125, 85, 70–1.

10. Prefaces to *The Princess Casamassima* and *The Portrait of a Lady* in Blackmur, *The Art of the Novel* (see note 9), pp.71, 46, 65, 51; Henry James, *What Maisie Knew* (1897; rpt. Harmondsworth: Penguin, 1977), p.194.

CHAPTER TWO

1. Virginia Woolf, *A Writer's Diary: Being extracts from the diary of Virginia Woolf*, ed. Leonard Woolf (1953; rpt. London: Triad, 1985), p.84.

2. T.S. Eliot, 'Ulysses, Order and Myth' (1923), rpt. in Frank Kermode (ed.), *Selected Prose of T.S. Eliot* (London: Faber and Faber, 1975), p.177.

3. Virginia Woolf, 'Modern Fiction' (1919), rpt. in *Collected Essays* (London: Hogarth Press, 1966), vol. II, pp.106–7.

4. Virginia Woolf, 'Character in Fiction', *The Essays of Virginia Woolf*, ed. Andrew McNeillie (London: Hogarth Press, 1988), vol. III, p.504.

5. D.H. Lawrence, letter of 5 June 1914, *The Collected Letters of D.H. Lawrence*, ed. Harry T. Moore (London: Heinemann, 1962), vol. I, p.282; D.H. Lawrence, *The Rainbow* (1915; rpt. Harmondsworth: Penguin, 1971), p.39, and *Women in Love* (1921; rpt. Harmondsworth: Penguin, 1971), p.221; D.H. Lawrence, *Fantasia of the Unconscious and Psychoanalysis and the Unconscious* (1923; rpt. London: Heinemann, 1961), p.11.

6. Henry James, 'The Future of the Novel' (1899), rpt. in Leon Edel and Gordon N. Ray (eds.), *Henry James and H.G. Wells* (London: Rupert Hart-Davis, 1958), p.57.

7. Dorothy Richardson, Foreword to *Pilgrimage* (1915–67; rpt. London: Virago, 1979), vol. I, p.9.

8. Virginia Woolf, *A Room of One's Own* (1929; rpt. Harmondsworth: Penguin, 1975), p.96.

9. William James, *The Principles of Psychology* (London: Macmillan, 1890), vol. I, p.239; May Sinclair, 'The Novels of Dorothy Richardson', *The Egoist*, April 1918, p.58.

10. Alan Friedman, 'The Novel', in C.B. Cox and A.E. Dyson (eds.), *The Twentieth Century Mind* (London: Oxford University Press,

1972), vol. I, p.442; James Joyce quoted in Frank Budgen, *James Joyce and the Making of Ulysses* (London: Grayson and Grayson, 1934), p.15.

11. Richardson, Foreword to *Pilgrimage* (see note 7), p.12.
12. Hugh Kenner, *Joyce's Voices* (London: Faber and Faber, 1978), p.xii.
13. Virginia Woolf, 'The Leaning Tower' (1940), rpt. in *Collected Essays* (see note 3), pp.167, 170; D.H. Lawrence, *Lady Chatterley's Lover* (1928; rpt. Harmondsworth: Penguin, 1982), p.5.
14. Virginia Woolf, 'Modern Fiction' (see note 3), p.106; Virginia Woolf, *A Writer's Diary* (see note 1), p.138.
15. Eugene Jolas, 'The Revolution of Language and James Joyce', in Samuel Beckett *et al.*, *Our Exagmination Round his Factification for Incamination of Work in Progress* (1929; rpt. London: Faber and Faber, 1972), p.79.
16. Walter Allen, *The English Novel: A short critical history* (London: Phoenix House, 1954), p.348.
17. Georg Lukács, 'The Ideology of Modernism' (1955), rpt. in David Lodge (ed.), *20th Century Literary Criticism: A reader* (London: Longman, 1972), pp.479, 484, 486.

CHAPTER THREE

1. Philip Henderson, *The Novel Today: Studies in contemporary attitudes* (London: John Lane, 1936), pp.81, 103, 52, 27.
2. Christopher Isherwood, *Lions and Shadows: An education in the twenties* (1938; rpt. London: Methuen, 1982), p.182.
3. *ibid.*, pp.52–3.
4. Virginia Woolf, 'The Leaning Tower' (1940), rpt. in *Collected Essays* (London: Hogarth Press, 1966), vol. II, p.172.
5. George Orwell, 'Inside the Whale' (1940), rpt. in Sonia Orwell and Ian Angus (eds.), *The Collected Essays, Journalism and Letters of George Orwell* (1968; rpt. Harmondsworth: Penguin, 1970), vol. I, p.557; George Orwell, 'Why I Write' (1946), rpt. in Orwell and Angus, vol. I, p.24.
6. Orwell, 'Why I Write' (see note 5), p.28.
7. George Orwell, letter to T.R. Fyvel, rpt. in Orwell and Angus, *The Collected Essays, Journalism and Letters of George Orwell*, (see note 5), vol. IV, p.558.
8. Graham Greene, 'God and Literature and So Forth', interview with Anthony Burgess, *The Observer*, 16 March 1980, p.33; Graham Greene, *Ways of Escape* (London: The Bodley Head, 1980), p.19.
9. Greene, *Ways of Escape* (see note 8), p.88.

10. In *A Sort of Life* (Harmondsworth: Penguin, 1972), p.85, Greene suggests that he would use these lines from Robert Browning's poem 'Bishop Blougram's Apology' if he were to choose an epigraph for all the novels he had written.
11. J.B. Priestley, Introduction to Patrick Hamilton, *Twenty Thousand Streets Under the Sky* (London: Constable, 1935), p.8.
12. Rex Warner, Author's Note to *The Aerodrome* (1941; rpt. Oxford: Oxford University Press, 1982).
13. Orwell, 'Inside the Whale' (see note 5), p.564.
14. Christopher Isherwood, Edward Upward, Evelyn Waugh, George Orwell, Graham Greene, Anthony Powell, and Henry Green all attended public school and – with the exception of Orwell – went on to university at Oxford or Cambridge.
15. Elizabeth Bowen, *English Novelists* (London: Collins, 1942), p.48.

CHAPTER FOUR

1. George Orwell, 'Inside the Whale' (1940); rpt. in Sonia Orwell and Ian Angus (eds.), *The Collected Essays, Journalism and Letters of George Orwell* (1968; rpt. Harmondsworth: Penguin, 1970), vol. I, p.578; P.H. Newby, *The Novel 1945–1950* (London: Longmans, Green and Co., 1951), p.13; Robert Hewison, *Under Siege* (London: Quartet Books, 1979), p.185.
2. Tom Harrisson, 'War Books', *Horizon*, December 1941, pp.435, 436; Henry Green, 'Mr. Jonas', *Penguin New Writing*, 1942, no.14, p.15.
3. Henry Green, 'A Novelist to his Readers – Communication without Speech', *The Listener*, 9 November 1950, p.506.
4. Rosamond Lehmann, 'The Future of the Novel?', *Britain Today*, June 1946, pp.6–7.
5. Walter Allen, *Tradition and Dream: The English and American novel from the twenties to our time* (London: Dent, 1964), p.262.
6. Lehmann, 'The Future of the Novel?' (see note 4), p.7; Newby, *The Novel 1945–1950* (see note 1), p.8.
7. Anthony Burgess, *Ninety-nine Novels: The best in English since 1939* (London: Allison and Busby, 1984), p.36.
8. Joyce Cary, 'Prefatory Essay' to *Herself Surprised* (1941; rpt. London: Michael Joseph, 1958), p.7.
9. Henry Reed, *The Novel since 1939* (London: Longmans, Green and Co., 1946), p.23.
10. Oh thou, that dear and happy isle
    The garden of the world ere while . . .
    What luckless apple did we taste,
    To make us mortal, and thee waste?

Stanza 41 of 'Upon Appleton House' in Andrew Marvell, *The Complete Poems*, ed. Elizabeth Story Donno (Harmondsworth: Penguin, 1972), p.85.

11. Malcolm Lowry, letter to Jonathan Cape, 2 January 1946, rpt. in Harvey Breit and Margerie Bonner Lowry, *Selected Letters of Malcolm Lowry* (1967; rpt. Harmondsworth: Penguin, 1985), p.66. Some recent Penguin editions of *Under the Volcano* reproduce this letter as an introduction to the novel.

12. *ibid.*, p.66.

13. P.H. Newby, *The Novel 1945–1950* (see note 1), p.14.

14. William Cooper, quoted in Rubin Rabinovitz, *The Reaction against Experiment in the English Novel, 1950–1960* (New York: Columbia University Press, 1967), p.6; C.P. Snow, 'Challenge to the Intellect', *Times Literary Supplement*, 15 August 1958, p.iii.

15. John Osborne, *Look Back in Anger* (1957; rpt. London: Faber, 1978), p.84.

CHAPTER FIVE

1. John Wain, interview with Frank Kermode, 'The House of Fiction' (1963), rpt. in Malcolm Bradbury (ed.), *The Novel Today* (Glasgow: Fontana, 1977), p.130.

2. Iris Murdoch, 'Against Dryness' (1961), rpt. in Bradbury, *The Novel Today* (see note 1), p.23.

3. Angus Wilson, 'Mood of the Month – III', *London Magazine*, April 1958, p.44; Malcolm Cowley (ed.), *Writers at Work: The 'Paris Review' interviews*, (London: Secker and Warburg, 1958) First series, p.231.

4. Malcolm Bradbury, *Possibilities: Essays on the state of the novel* (London: Oxford University Press, 1973), p.211.

5. 'The State of Fiction: A symposium', *The New Review*, Summer 1978, p.39.

6. *ibid.*, p.65.

7. Margaret Drabble in James Vinson (ed.), *Contemporary Novelists* (London: St James Press, 1976), 2nd edn, p.373.

8. *The New Review* symposium (see note 5), p.51.

9. Ihab Hassan, *The Postmodern Turn: Essays in postmodern theory and culture* (Lincoln, Ohio: Ohio State University Press, 1987), pp.xiii–xiv.

10. A suggestion Durrell accepts in his interview in Malcolm Cowley (ed.), *Writers at Work: The 'Paris Review' interviews* (London: Secker and Warburg, 1963), Second series, p.231.

11. Alain Robbe-Grillet, *Snapshots and Towards a New Novel*, trans. Barbara Wright (London: Calder and Boyars, 1965), pp.46–7, 63.

12. David Lodge, *The Novelist at the Crossroads and Other Essays on Fiction and Criticism* (London: Routledge and Kegan Paul, 1971), pp.18, 22.
13. Doris Lessing, 'The Small Personal Voice' in Tom Maschler (ed.), *Declaration* (London: MacGibbon and Kee, 1957), p.14.
14. Anthony Burgess, *The Novel Now* (London: Faber, 1971), p.192.
15. Malcolm Bradbury, Foreword to Jay L. Halio (ed.), *Dictionary of Literary Biography*, vol. 14, *British Novelists since 1960* (Detroit: Gale Research, 1983), vol. I, p.xvi.
16. David Lodge in Vinson, *Contemporary Novelists* (see note 7), p.833.
17. David Lodge, 'The Novelist: Still at the crossroads?', lecture to the British Council Cambridge Seminar, 'The Contemporary British Writer', Christ's College, Cambridge, 11 July 1991.
18. *The New Review* symposium (see note 5), p.18.
19. Bradbury, Foreword to *Dictionary of Literary Biography* (see note 15), p.xviii.

CHAPTER SIX

1. Graham Greene, *Ways of Escape* (London: The Bodley Head, 1980), p.95; Anthony Burgess in conversation with Edna O'Brien and Clive James in 'The Late Clive James', Channel Four Television, 11 May 1985.
2. Anthony Burgess, *The Novel Now* (London: Faber, 1971), p.19.
3. Farrell's remark is quoted in a note to the Penguin edition of his novels.
4. Burgess, *The Novel Now* (see note 2), p.165.
5. 'The State of Fiction: A symposium', *The New Review*, Summer 1978, p.65.
6. David Lodge, *The Novelist at the Crossroads and Other Essays on Fiction and Criticism* (London: Routledge and Kegan Paul, 1971), p.9.
7. Salman Rushdie, 'The Location of *Brazil*' (1985), rpt. in *Imaginary Homelands: Essays and criticism 1981–1991* (London: Granta Books, 1991), pp.124–5.
8. Virginia Woolf, *A Room of One's Own* (1929; rpt. Harmondsworth: Penguin, 1975), p.96.
9. Mikhail Bakhtin, *The Dialogic Imagination: Four essays*, ed. Michael Holquist, trans. Michael Holquist and Caryl Emerson (Austin, Texas: University of Texas Press, 1981), p.47.
10. Virginia Woolf, 'Mr. Bennett and Mrs. Brown' (1924), rpt. in *Collected Essays* (London: Hogarth Press, 1966), vol. I, p.337.

Bibliography

I FICTION

The list which follows does not attempt to provide an exhaustive catalogue of the best fiction in the twentieth century. Instead, it notes year-by-year all the novels mentioned in this study: for those from which quotations appear in the text, details are also included of the editions used (where possible, recent paperbacks).

1900

Joseph Conrad *Lord Jim* (Harmondsworth: Penguin, 1968)
Joseph Conrad and Ford Madox Ford *The Inheritors*

1901

George Douglas Brown *The House with the Green Shutters*
Rudyard Kipling *Kim*
H.G. Wells *The First Men in the Moon*

1902

Arnold Bennett *Anna of the Five Towns* (Harmondsworth: Penguin, 1976)
Joseph Conrad *Heart of Darkness* (First published 1899. Harmondsworth: Penguin, 1983)

1903

Samuel Butler *The Way of all Flesh*
Erskine Childers *The Riddle of the Sands*

Joseph Conrad and Ford Madox Ford *Romance*
Henry James *The Ambassadors*

1904

Joseph Conrad *Nostromo* (Harmondsworth: Penguin, 1969)
John Galsworthy *The Island Pharisees*
Guy Thorne *When it was Dark* (London: Greening and Co., 1904)

1905

H.G. Wells *Kipps* (London: Fontana, 1973)

1906

John Galsworthy *The Forsyte Saga*:
  A Man of Property (1906; rpt. London: Heinemann, 1929)
  In Chancery (1920)
  To Let (1921)
  A Modern Comedy (1929)
William Le Queux *The Invasion of 1910* (London: Eveleigh Nash, 1906)
H.G. Wells *In the Days of the Comet*

1907

Joseph Conrad *The Secret Agent*
Edmund Gosse *Father and Son*
Elizabeth Robins *The Convert*

1908

Arnold Bennett *The Old Wives' Tale* (London: Pan, 1980)
E.M. Forster *A Room with a View*

1909

H.G. Wells *Ann Veronica*
H.G. Wells *Tono-Bungay* (London: Pan, 1972)

1910

Arnold Bennett *Clayhanger* series:
  Clayhanger (1910)

Hilda Lessways (1911)
These Twain (1916)
The Roll Call (1918)
John Buchan *Prester John*
E.M. Forster *Howards End*
H.G. Wells *The History of Mr Polly*

1911

Joseph Conrad *Under Western Eyes*

1912

Arthur Conan Doyle *The Lost World*

1913

Joseph Conrad *Chance* (Harmondsworth: Penguin, 1984)
D.H. Lawrence *Sons and Lovers*
Compton Mackenzie *Sinister Street* (1913–14)

1914

J. McDougall Hay *Gillespie*

1915

John Buchan *The Thirty-Nine Steps*
Ford Madox Ford *The Good Soldier* (Harmondsworth: Penguin, 1977)
D.H. Lawrence *The Rainbow* (Harmondsworth: Penguin, 1971)
John Cowper Powys *Wood and Stone*
Dorothy Richardson *Pilgrimage* (London: Virago, 1979; 4 vols.):
Pointed Roofs (1915)
Backwater (1916)
Honeycomb (1917)
The Tunnel (1919)
Interim (1919)
Deadlock (1921)
Revolving Lights (1923)
The Trap (1925)
Oberland (1927)
Dawn's Left Hand (1931)

Clear Horizon (1935)
Dimple Hill (1938)
March Moonlight (1967)

1916

James Joyce *A Portrait of the Artist as a Young Man* (Harmondsworth: Penguin, 1971)

1917

Norman Douglas *South Wind*

1918

Wyndham Lewis *Tarr* (Harmondsworth: Penguin, 1982)

1919

Ronald Firbank *Valmouth*
May Sinclair *Mary Olivier* (London: Virago, 1980)

1920

D.H. Lawrence *The Lost Girl*

1921

Aldous Huxley *Crome Yellow*
D.H. Lawrence *Women in Love* (Harmondsworth: Penguin, 1971)

1922

James Joyce *Ulysses* (Harmondsworth: Penguin, 1992)

1923

Aldous Huxley *Antic Hay*
D.H. Lawrence *Kangaroo* (Harmondsworth: Penguin, 1981)

1924

Ronald Firbank *Sorrow in Sunlight*
Ford Madox Ford *Parade's End*:

Some Do Not . . . (1924)
No More Parades (1925)
A Man Could Stand Up – (1926)
The Last Post (1928)
E.M. Forster *A Passage to India*

1925

Ivy Compton-Burnett *Pastors and Masters*
Virginia Woolf *Mrs Dalloway* (Harmondsworth: Penguin, 1976)

1926

Ronald Firbank *Concerning the Eccentricities of Cardinal Pirelli*

1927

T.F. Powys *Mr Weston's Good Wine*
Henry Williamson *Tarka the Otter*
Virginia Woolf *To the Lighthouse* (Harmondsworth: Penguin, 1973)

1928

Aldous Huxley *Point Counter Point*
Christopher Isherwood *All the Conspirators* (London: Methuen, 1984)
D.H. Lawrence *Lady Chatterley's Lover* (Harmondsworth: Penguin, 1982)
Wyndham Lewis *The Childermass*
Evelyn Waugh *Decline and Fall*
Virginia Woolf *Orlando* (Harmondsworth: Penguin, 1975)

1929

Richard Aldington *Death of a Hero* (London: Hogarth Press, 1984)
Henry Green *Living*
Graham Greene *The Man Within*
Richard Hughes *A High Wind in Jamaica*
L.H. Myers *The Near and the Far*:
   The Near and the Far (1929)
   Prince Jali (1931)
   The Root and the Flower (1935)
   The Pool of Vishnu (1940)
John Cowper Powys *Wolf Solent*
P.G. Wodehouse *Summer Lightning*

1930

Graham Greene *The Name of Action*
Wyndham Lewis *The Apes of God*
W. Somerset Maugham *Cakes and Ale*
J.B. Priestley *Angel Pavement*
Evelyn Waugh *Vile Bodies*
Henry Williamson *A Patriot's Progress*

1931

Graham Greene *Rumour at Nightfall*
Eric Linklater *Juan in America*
Naomi Mitchison *The Corn King and the Spring Queen*
Anthony Powell *Afternoon Men*
Virginia Woolf *The Waves* (Harmondsworth: Penguin, 1973)

1932

Lewis Grassic Gibbon *A Scots Quair* (London: Pan, 1982):
    Sunset Song (1932)
    Cloud Howe (1933)
    Grey Granite (l934)
Graham Greene *Stamboul Train*
Aldous Huxley *Brave New World*
Christoper Isherwood *The Memorial* (London: Panther, 1978)
Rosamond Lehmann *Invitation to the Waltz*
John Cowper Powys *A Glastonbury Romance*
Evelyn Waugh *Black Mischief*

1933

Walter Greenwood *Love on the Dole*
Malcolm Lowry *Ultramarine*

1934

Graham Greene *It's a Battlefield* (Harmondsworth: Penguin, 1978)
Eric Linklater *Magnus Merriman*
John Cowper Powys *Weymouth Sands*
Evelyn Waugh *A Handful of Dust*

1935

Elizabeth Bowen *The House in Paris* (Harmondsworth: Penguin, 1983)
Ivy Compton-Burnett *A House and its Head*

Graham Greene *England Made Me*
Patrick Hamilton *Twenty Thousand Streets Under the Sky*
Christopher Isherwood *Mr Norris Changes Trains* (London: Panther, 1977)
George Orwell *A Clergyman's Daughter* (Harmondsworth: Penguin, 1982)

1936

William Gerhardie *Of Mortal Love*
Graham Greene *A Gun for Sale*
Rosamond Lehmann *The Weather in the Streets* (London: Virago, 1981)
George Orwell *Keep the Aspidistra Flying*
John Cowper Powys *Maiden Castle*

1937

Neil Gunn *Highland River*
Wyndham Lewis *The Revenge for Love* (London: Secker and Warburg, 1982)
Compton Mackenzie *The Four Winds of Love* (8 vols.; 1937–45)
Rex Warner *The Wild Goose Chase*

1938

Samuel Beckett *Murphy*
Elizabeth Bowen *The Death of the Heart*
Lawrence Durrell *The Black Book*
Graham Greene *Brighton Rock*
C.S. Lewis *Out of the Silent Planet*
Edward Upward *Journey to the Border* (London: Hogarth Press, 1938)
Evelyn Waugh *Scoop*

1939

James Barke *The Land of the Leal*
Joyce Cary *Mister Johnson*
Graham Greene *The Confidential Agent* (Harmondsworth: Penguin, 1967)
Christopher Isherwood *Goodbye to Berlin* (London: Granada, 1983)
Lewis Jones *We Live*
James Joyce *Finnegans Wake* (London: Faber, 1971)
Flann O'Brien *At Swim-Two-Birds* (Harmondsworth: Penguin, 1975)
George Orwell *Coming up for Air* (Harmondsworth: Penguin, 1962)
Jean Rhys *Good Morning, Midnight*

1940

Graham Greene *The Power and the Glory*
Arthur Koestler *Darkness at Noon*
C.P. Snow *Strangers and Brothers*:
  George Passant (1940)
  The Light and the Dark (1947)
  Time of Hope (1949)
  The Masters (1951)
  The New Men (1954)
  Homecomings (1956)
  The Conscience of the Rich (1956)
  The Affair (1960)
  Corridors of Power (1964)
  The Sleep of Reason (1968)
  Last Things (1970)

1941

Joyce Cary *Triptych* (Harmondsworth: Penguin, 1985):
  Herself Surprised (1941)
  To be a Pilgrim (1942)
  The Horse's Mouth (1944)
Rex Warner *The Aerodrome* (Oxford: Oxford University Press, 1982)
Virginia Woolf *Between the Acts* (London: Panther, 1978)

1942

Evelyn Waugh *Put out More Flags* (Harmondsworth: Penguin, 1973)

1943

Henry Green *Caught* (London: Hogarth Press, 1978)
James Hanley *No Directions*
C.S. Lewis *Voyage to Venus* (London: Pan, 1953)

1944

L.P. Hartley *Eustace and Hilda*:
  The Shrimp and the Anemone (1944)
  The Sixth Heaven (1946)
  Eustace and Hilda (1947)
Rosamond Lehmann *The Ballad and the Source* (London: Virago, 1982)
W. Somerset Maugham *The Razor's Edge*

1945

Henry Green *Loving*
C.S. Lewis *That Hideous Strength*
George Orwell *Animal Farm*
Evelyn Waugh *Brideshead Revisited* (Harmondsworth: Penguin, 1972)

1946

Henry Green *Back*
Eric Linklater *Private Angelo*
Mervyn Peake *The Titus Books* (Harmondsworth: Penguin, 1983):
  Titus Groan (1946)
  Gormenghast (1950)
  Titus Alone (1959)

1947

Malcolm Lowry *Under the Volcano* (Harmondsworth: Penguin, 1983)

1948

Alexander Baron *From the City, From the Plough*
Henry Green *Concluding*
Graham Greene *The Heart of the Matter*
Aldous Huxley *Ape and Essence*
Evelyn Waugh *The Loved One*

1949

Elizabeth Bowen *The Heat of the Day* (Harmondsworth: Penguin, 1983)
George Orwell *Nineteen Eighty-Four*

1950

William Cooper *Scenes from Provincial Life*
Henry Green *Nothing*

1951

Graham Greene *The End of the Affair* (Harmondsworth: Penguin, 1976)
Anthony Powell *A Dance to the Music of Time*:
  A Question of Upbringing (1951)

A Buyer's Market (1952; rpt. London: Fontana, 1980)
The Acceptance World (1955; rpt. London: Fontana, 1983)
At Lady Molly's (1957)
Casanova's Chinese Restaurant (1960)
The Kindly Ones (1962)
The Valley of Bones (1964)
The Soldier's Art (1966)
The Military Philosophers (1968)
Books do Furnish a Room (1971)
Temporary Kings (1973)
Hearing Secret Harmonies (1975)
Henry Williamson *A Chronicle of Ancient Sunlight*:
The Dark Lantern (1951; rpt. London: Zenith, 1984)
Donkey Boy (1952)
Young Phillip Maddison (1953)
How Dear is Life (1954)
A Fox under my Cloak (1955)
The Golden Virgin (1957)
Love and the Loveless (1958)
A Test to Destruction (1960)
The Innocent Moon (1961)
It was the Nightingale (1962)
The Power of the Dead (1963)
The Phoenix Generation (1965)
A Solitary War (1966)
Lucifer before Sunrise (1967)
The Gale of the World (1969)

1952

Joyce Cary *Prisoner of Grace*
Henry Green *Doting*
Doris Lessing *Children of Violence*:
Martha Quest (1952)
A Proper Marriage (1954)
A Ripple from the Storm (1958)
Landlocked (1965)
The Four-Gated City (1969)
P.H. Newby *A Step to Silence* (London: Cape, 1952)
William Plomer *Museum Pieces* (Harmondsworth: Penguin, 1961)
Evelyn Waugh *Sword of Honour* (Harmondsworth: Penguin, 1984):
Men at Arms (1952)
Officers and Gentlemen (1955)
Unconditional Surrender (1961)

1953

Joyce Cary *Except the Lord*
Ian Fleming *Casino Royale*
L.P. Hartley *The Go-Between* (Harmondsworth: Penguin, 1983)
P.H. Newby *The Retreat* (London: Cape, 1953)
John Wain *Hurry on Down*

1954

Kingsley Amis *Lucky Jim*
William Golding *Lord of the Flies* (London: Faber, 1967)
Iris Murdoch *Under the Net* (London: Granada, 1983)
J.R.R. Tolkien *The Lord of the Rings*:
    The Fellowship of the Ring (1954)
    The Two Towers (1954)
    The Return of the King (1955)

1955

Joyce Cary *Not Honour More*
Nigel Dennis *Cards of Identity*
J.P. Donleavy *The Ginger Man*
William Golding *The Inheritors*
Graham Greene *The Quiet American*
Wyndham Lewis *Monstre Gai*
Wyndham Lewis *Malign Fiesta* (London: John Calder, 1965)

1956

Anthony Burgess *The Long Day Wanes* (*The Malayan Trilogy*):
    Time for a Tiger (1956)
    The Enemy in the Blanket (1958)
    Beds in the East (1959)
William Golding *Pincher Martin*
Angus Wilson *Anglo-Saxon Attitudes* (Harmondsworth: Penguin, 1976)

1957

John Braine *Room at the Top*
Lawrence Durrell *The Alexandria Quartet* (London: Faber, 1974):
    Justine (1957)
    Balthazar (1958)

Mountolive (1958)
Clea (1960)
Colin MacInnes 'London Novels':
  City of Spades (1957)
  Absolute Beginners (1959)
  Mr Love and Justice (1960)
Nevil Shute *On the Beach*
Muriel Spark *The Comforters* (Harmondsworth: Penguin, 1978)

1958

Chinua Achebe *Things Fall Apart*
John Bowen *After the Rain*
Graham Greene *Our Man in Havana*
Alan Sillitoe *Saturday Night and Sunday Morning*

1959

Samuel Beckett 'The Beckett Trilogy' (London: Picador, 1983):
  Molloy (1950)
  Malone Dies (1951)
  The Unnamable (1952; trans. 1959)

1960

Kingsley Amis *Take a Girl Like You*
Stan Barstow *A Kind of Loving*
Wilson Harris *Palace of the Peacocks*
L.P. Hartley *Facial Justice*
Olivia Manning *The Balkan Trilogy* (Harmondsworth: Penguin, 1982):
  The Great Fortune (1960)
  The Spoilt City (1962)
  Friends and Heroes (1965)
David Storey *This Sporting Life*

1961

Richard Hughes *The Fox in the Attic*
Iris Murdoch *A Severed Head*
V.S. Naipaul *A House for Mr Biswas*
Muriel Spark *The Prime of Miss Jean Brodie* (Harmondsworth: Penguin, 1982)
Angus Wilson *The Old Men at the Zoo*

1962

Anthony Burgess *A Clockwork Orange*
Gabriel Fielding *The Birthday King* (London: Hutchinson, 1962)
Rayner Heppenstall *The Connecting Door*
Doris Lessing *The Golden Notebook* (London: Granada, 1972)
Edward Upward *In the Thirties*

1963

John Le Carré *The Spy who Came in from the Cold*

1964

B.S. Johnson *Albert Angelo*
Julian Mitchell *The White Father* (London: Constable, 1964)
Angus Wilson *Late Call* (London: Granada, 1982)

1965

Malcolm Bradbury *Stepping Westward*
Margaret Drabble *The Millstone* (Harmondsworth: Penguin, 1981)
David Lodge *The British Museum is Falling Down*
Jean Rhys *Wide Sargasso Sea*

1966

John Fowles *The Magus*
Graham Greene *The Comedians*
Edna O'Brien *Casualties of Peace*
Paul Scott *The Raj Quartet*:
    The Jewel in the Crown (1966)
    The Day of the Scorpion (1968)
    The Towers of Silence (1971)
    A Division of the Spoils (1975)

1967

Andrew Sinclair *Gog*
Christina Stead *Cotter's England*
Angus Wilson *No Laughing Matter*

1968

Brian Aldiss *Report on Probability A*
Thomas Hinde *High*
Julian Mitchell *The Undiscovered Country*
P.H. Newby *Something to Answer For*

1969

Brigid Brophy *In Transit*
Margaret Drabble *The Waterfall*
John Fowles *The French Lieutenant's Woman* (London: Panther, 1977)
B.S. Johnson *The Unfortunates*

1970

Iris Murdoch *A Fairly Honourable Defeat*
Muriel Spark *The Driver's Seat*

1971

David Caute *The Occupation*
Susan Hill *Strange Meeting*
B.S. Johnson *House Mother Normal*
Fay Weldon *Down Among the Women* (Harmondsworth: Penguin, 1983)

1972

John Berger *G.*
Christine Brooke-Rose *Thru*
Angela Carter *The Infernal Desire Machines of Doctor Hoffman* (Harmonds-
    worth: Penguin, 1982)
David Storey *Pasmore*

1973

J.G. Farrell *The Siege of Krishnapur* (Harmondsworth: Penguin, 1983)
Richard Hughes *The Wooden Shepherdess*
B.S. Johnson *Christie Malry's Own Double Entry*
Doris Lessing *The Summer before the Dark*
Iris Murdoch *The Black Prince*

1974

Beryl Bainbridge *The Bottle Factory Outing*

1975

Malcolm Bradbury *The History Man*
Ruth Prawer Jhabvala *Heat and Dust*
David Lodge *Changing Places*

1976

Beryl Bainbridge *A Quiet Life*

1977

Margaret Drabble *The Ice Age* (Harmondsworth: Penguin, 1983)
Rayner Heppenstall *Two Moons*
Olivia Manning *The Levant Trilogy*:
    The Danger Tree (1977)
    The Battle Lost and Won (1978)
    The Sum of Things (1980)
William McIlvanney *Laidlaw*
Paul Scott *Staying On* (London: Granada, 1983)

1978

J.G. Farrell *The Singapore Grip*
Graham Greene *The Human Factor*
Ian McEwan *The Cement Garden*
Iris Murdoch *The Sea, the Sea*
Emma Tennant *The Bad Sister* (London: Picador, 1979)

1979

J.G. Ballard *The Unlimited Dream Company*
William Golding *Darkness Visible* (London: Faber, 1980)
Doris Lessing *Canopus in Argos: Archives* series:
    Re: Colonised Planet 5, Shikasta (1979)
    The Marriages between Zones Three, Four and Five (1980)
    The Sirian Experiments (1981)
    The Making of the Representative for Planet 8 (1982)
    Documents Relating to the Sentimental Agents in the Volyen Empire (1983)

1980

Anthony Burgess *Earthly Powers* (Harmondsworth: Penguin, 1981)
J.L. Carr *A Month in the Country*

William Golding *To the Ends of the Earth*: *A Sea Trilogy*:
  Rites of Passage (London: Faber, 1982)
  Close Quarters (1987)
  Fire Down Below (1989)
John Le Carré *Smiley's People*

1981

Martin Amis *Other People* (Harmondsworth: Penguin, 1982)
Paul Bailey *Old Soldiers*
Eva Figes *Waking* (London: Hamish Hamilton, 1981)
Alasdair Gray *Lanark* (London: Granada, 1982)
Salman Rushdie *Midnight's Children* (London: Picador, 1982)
D.M. Thomas *The White Hotel*

1982

Anita Brookner *Providence*
Graham Greene *Monsignor Quixote*
Kazuo Ishiguro *A Pale View of the Hills*
Thomas Keneally *Schindler's Ark*

1983

Malcolm Bradbury *Rates of Exchange* (London: Arena, 1984)
Graham Swift *Waterland*

1984

Martin Amis *Money*
J.G. Ballard *Empire of the Sun*
Julian Barnes *Flaubert's Parrot*
Alasdair Gray *1982, Janine*

1985

Keri Hulme *The Bone People*

1986

Peter Ackroyd *Hawksmoor*
Ian Banks *The Bridge*
Kazuo Ishiguro *An Artist of the Floating World*
Timothy Mo *An Insular Possession*

1987

Brian Aldiss *Ruins*
Ron Butlin *The Sound of my Voice*

1988

Peter Carey *Oscar and Lucinda*

1989

Martin Amis *London Fields*
Kazuo Ishiguro *The Remains of the Day*
James Kelman *A Disaffection*
Caryl Phillips *Higher Ground*
Jeanette Winterson *Sexing the Cherry*

1990

A.S. Byatt *Possession*
Brian McCabe *The Other McCoy*

1991

Ben Okri *The Famished Road* (London: Vintage, 1992)
Caryl Phillips *Cambridge*

1992

Andrew Greig *Electric Brae*
Ian McEwan *The Black Dogs*

II BACKGROUND AND CRITICAL

Works relating to individual periods or phases of development are
listed in the sections of *Further Reading* at the end of each chapter. The
list below contains more general introductions and bibliographies
relevant to the twentieth century as a whole, or to broader areas within
it.

Allen, Walter *Tradition and Dream: The English and American novel from the
    twenties to our time*, London: Dent, 1964.

Atkins, John *The British Spy Novel: Styles in treachery*, London: John Calder, 1984.

Bergonzi, Bernard (ed.) *Sphere History of Literature in the English Language*, vol. 7, *The Twentieth Century*, London: Sphere, 1970.

Biles, Jack I. (ed.) *British Novelists since 1900*, New York: AMS, 1987.

Blamires, Harry *Twentieth Century English Literature*, London: Macmillan, 1982.

Bradbury, Malcolm *Possibilities: Essays on the state of the novel*, London: Oxford University Press, 1973.

Bradbury, Malcolm *No, Not Bloomsbury*, London: Andre Deutsch, 1987.

Breen, Jennifer *In her own Write: Twentieth-century women's fiction*, London: Macmillan, 1990.

Bufkin, E.C. *The Twentieth-Century Novel in English: A checklist*, Georgia: University of Georgia Press, 1984.

Burgess, Anthony *The Novel Now: A student's guide to contemporary fiction*, London: Faber, 1971.

Burgess, Anthony *Ninety-nine Novels: The best in English since 1939*, London: Allison and Busby, 1984.

Cahalan, James M. *The Irish Novel: A critical history*, Boston: Twayne, 1988.

Cockburn, Claud *Bestseller: The books that everyone read 1900–1939*, London: Sidgwick and Jackson, 1972.

Craig, Cairns (ed.) *The History of Scottish Literature*: vol. 4, *Twentieth Century*, Aberdeen: Aberdeen University Press, 1987.

Crossland, Margaret *Beyond the Lighthouse: English women novelists in the twentieth century*, London: Constable, 1981.

Ford, Boris (ed.) *The New Pelican Guide to English Literature*, vol.7, *From James to Eliot*, Harmondsworth: Penguin, 1983a.

Ford, Boris (ed.) *The New Pelican Guide to English Literature*, vol. 8, *The Present Age*, Harmondsworth: Penguin, 1983b.

Friedman, Alan Warren *Forms of Modern British Fiction*, Austin and London: University of Texas Press, 1975.

Hart, Francis *The Scottish Novel: A critical survey*, London: John Murray, 1978.

Hawthorn, Jeremy (ed.) *The British Working-Class Novel in the Twentieth Century*, London: Edward Arnold, 1984.

Henderson, Lesley (ed.) *Contemporary Novelists*, Chicago and London: St James Press, 1991.

Hewitt, Douglas *English Fiction of the Early Modern Period, 1890–1940*, London: Longman, 1989.

Higdon, David Leon *Shadows of the Past in Contemporary British Fiction*, London: Macmillan, 1984.

Kettle, Arnold *An Introduction to the English Novel* vol. 2, *Henry James to 1950*, London: Hutchinson, 1967.

Maes-Jelinek, Hena *Criticism of Society in the English Novel Between the Wars*, Paris: Société d'Editions 'Les Belles Lettres', 1970.

McHale, Brian *Postmodernist Fiction*, London: Methuen, 1987.

Oldsey, Bernard *Dictionary of Literary Biography*, vol. 15, *British Novelists 1930–1959*, Detroit: Gale Research, 1983.

Orr, John *The Making of the Twentieth-Century Novel: Lawrence, Joyce, Faulkner and beyond*, London: Macmillan, 1987.

Rice, Thomas Jackson *English Fiction 1900–1950: General bibliography and individual authors*, 2 vols. Detroit: Gale Research, 1979.

Robson, W.W. *Modern English Literature*, London: Oxford University Press, 1970.

Schwarz, Daniel R. *The Transformation of the English Novel 1890–1930*, London: Macmillan, 1989.

Smith, Curtis C. (ed.) *Twentieth-Century Science Fiction Writers*, London: St James Press, 1986.

Smyth, Edmund *Postmodernism and Contemporary Fiction*, London: Batsford, 1991.

Staley, Thomas F. *Twentieth-Century Women Novelists*, London: Macmillan, 1982.

Stevenson, Lionel *The History of the English Novel*, vol. 11, *Yesterday and After*, New York: Barnes and Noble, 1967.

Stevenson, Randall *The British Novel since the Thirties: An introduction*, London: Batsford, 1986.

Stevenson, Randall *The British Novel in the Twentieth Century: An introductory bibliography*, London: British Council, 1988.

Swatridge, Colin *British Fiction: A student's A–Z*, London: Macmillan, 1985.

Swinden, Patrick *The English Novel of History and Society, 1940–1980*, London: Macmillan, 1984.

Vinson, James (ed.) *Twentieth Century Fiction*, London: Macmillan, 1983.

Index